Happy Reading

Audrey Malone

Betsy Ames MacFarland
105 Oxford Road
Oxford, Maryland 21654

THE HOPE TOWN READER

Selected Writings of the Hope Town Writers' Circle

The First Five Years
2000-2005

Compiled and Edited by Janet Pearce Foster

Indigo Ink Publishing
East Boothbay, Maine

INDIGO INK PUBLISHING
920 Ocean Point Road
East Boothbay, Maine 04544
USA
SAN 851-9331

This first edition was published September 2006 and is an original paperback.

THE HOPE TOWN READER.
Selected Writings of the Hope Town Writers' Circle
The First Five Years
2000-2005
Compiled and Edited by Janet Pearce Foster

Copyright 2006 by Indigo Ink Publishing

ISBN   978-0-9789106-0-0 (Original Paperback)
0-9789106-0-5

COVER ILLUSTRATION: The watercolor *Elbow Reef Lightstation* by Robert Chapman Foster III was painted from an Albury 20 during a visit with our gracious friends Dave and Phoebe Gale. The lighthouse is an icon for all those who love the Abacos.

This book was printed using Goudy Old Style typeface, designed in 1915 by Frederic W. Goudy.

THE HOPE TOWN READER
Selected Works by Members of
The Hope Town Writers' Circle
2000-2005

Foreword

This book has been several years in the making. The writings bear a common thread; while the Hope Town Writers' Circle produces works in a variety of formats and subjects, only those specific to the Abacos were selected. If the author provided a date, it has been included.

It is important to note that members of the Writers' Circle who were schooled in the British system and/or are native Bahamians adhere to the British spellings. With the exception of proper names, all others use the American forms. This is to explain the occurrence of both British spellings and American usage.

JPF
East Boothbay, Maine
August 2006

ACKNOWLEDGMENTS

My thanks go to all participants of the Hope Town Writers' Circle, especially to Audrey Malone. Her quiet nature and humility belies her talent. In Audrey, truly, still waters run deep; her character, composure and courage are an inspiration to me and to many others whose sentiment may be hidden.

Additionally, I am indebted to Mary Balzac who willingly became the conduit during the compilation of this book. At the outset, it was not clear how the project would be accomplished but Mary kept me focused and provided the incentive and information needed to complete the volume.

JPF

July 2006

Poet of Merit
(Or, How the Hope Town Writers' Circle Began)
Beti Web

It all began in the liquor store.

When we went in to refresh our supply of rum and Kalik. Audrey was alone and examining a beribboned medallion of Olympic proportions and grandeur.

"What is that?" asked my husband.

"It's the Poet of Merit medal presented to me in Washington for winning their annual international competition," she replied.

She went on to tell us that she had never before entered a literary competition but as she was struggling to come to terms with the loss of her only son, Benjie, she spotted a newspaper advertisement for the competition and decided to put her feelings down on paper. The words seemed to flow and, on impulse, she sealed the envelope, posted it and expected to hear no more.

We were thrilled but amazed to find that Audrey had kept news of her remarkable success completely to herself. In contrast, we felt we had to share the good news and it was not very long before several of us decided we had to do something to honour Audrey. I know only too well how difficult it is to get a mere mention in the 'Also Commended' category, let alone to be declared the winner of such a prestigious trophy. To be invited to Washington to read the poem before a large audience - WOW! I have also learned that poems about bereavement that are frequently written rarely win literary competitions and if they do it is because they are especially moving and well written. As we read Audrey's poem, we were deeply touched and understood exactly why she had won.

It was decided to make an open invitation to a meeting to honour Audrey. The commodore agreed that the meeting be held at the Hope Town Sailing Club. A supporting cast was arranged with Steve Best reading some of his engaging *Tales of Soleil and Sparkle*, whose penetrating insights into Hope Town social life have now been published. I read my narrative poem *The Candy Striped Lighthouse*.

Firstly, the meeting had to be advertised, describing the purpose of the event. We pinned the notices up on posts and fences around the Settlement suggesting that the meeting might also interest people who enjoyed writing in any of its forms. It occurred to us that this might be the occasion to find out whether there was sufficient interest in starting a writers' circle.

On the appointed day the coffee and biscuits stood ready on a table and audience chairs were appropriately placed. To our surprise, the room was packed.

Audrey stood at the table and after telling us how she came to win her award she read the poem to great applause.

I persuaded my husband to put forward the proposal to form a writers' circle. This was welcomed with enthusiasm and we asked those interested to sign up. There was to be no formal structure with no chairperson, no committee, no rules and most importantly, no subscription. The meetings would be weekly and would go on as long as the initial enthusiasm was maintained.

With a constantly changing island population, attendance at meetings can vary from 5-6 to more than twenty. Sometimes our best meetings have been quite small. Even by the end of the summer, that enthusiasm never fails and only with great reluctance do we take a short break as the hurricane season opens. We reopen as the winter residents return in the fall. One of our great delights is to see new faces as the 'Harbour Rats' provide fresh talent from cruising boats in the harbour.

We commissioned a logo for the group that declares our presence in the Sailing Club on Thursday mornings. It consists of a hand fashioned in the shape of Elbow Cay and holds our familiar lighthouse as a pen.

The main purpose of the writers' circle is so members write a piece that interests them. They can also give a sample of ongoing work of any kind to read to the members for positive critical comment or acclaim. Anyone may join the group. The interesting result is that the group has attracted people from all walks of life and from many different places to write about highly diverse subjects. As I also belong to a writers' group in England, it was recently suggested that the members of each group write on a given subject and exchange these; this has been enjoyable and enlightening.

One thing is certain: that the present participants are delighted that Audrey Malone's impulse provoked this added dimension to our time in Hope Town. Surely Wyannie Malone can look down on her descendent with pride and a benevolent smile.

April 2004

INTRODUCTION
Audrey Malone

Our Hope Town Writers' Circle began four years ago. After my son's death, I had some things I wanted to say to him. For years I had been reading about poetry contests and always intended to write something. One evening when things weren't going so well I picked up a magazine, saw the ad then sat down and wrote a poem to my son about what I was feeling, put it in an envelope and mailed it the next morning.

They liked my poem and published it in their annual anthology and invited me to Washington D.C. to receive a Poet of Merit Award. After I returned, some of my friends put together a celebration for me. We met a few weeks later and our Hope Town Writers' Circle began.

It keeps getting better with each meeting; we keep learning every week. Some of us have written things we never expected to write; we've laughed together, cried together, learned about each other and formed lasting friendships through our writings. Some of us have gone on to publish in magazines and some have published their own book. We have welcomed some well-known writers to our group during the years and learned a lot from them.

SON

My son, I miss you so
I hear your voice
When I awake each morning
But your chair is empty
My tears roll down my face
I know you don't want me to cry
But you were my only child
And you were so young to go
Your life not halfway finished
I had so many dreams for you
And I know you had dreams too
Nighttime comes, I hear your voice
Saying, I'll be home soon
I cry again, I miss you so.

HOPE TOWN AND ENVIRONS

MY FIRST VISIT TO HOPE TOWN
Nan Kenyon

"Now remember, if you hear the pumps stop, get out on deck with your life jackets on!"

What pumps? Which deck? Where are our life jackets? All of these questions and more were swirling around in my head as I stood on Potter's Cay pier that May afternoon in 1961. My husband of two months, Harry, and I were preparing to board the M/V *Stede Bonnet*, a 120´ converted minesweeper/mail boat, for her round trip from Nassau to Green Turtle Cay, Abaco, with stops at all of the settlements in between. This trip was to be the second part of our honeymoon, the first being a cruise to Spanish Wells on our Bahamian-built motorsailer, *Spindrift*, our new 28´ home.

Harry had been hired by the Bahamas Ministry of Tourism as the new editor of the Yachtsman's Guide to the Bahamas, and we had decided it would be a perfect time to begin our life together. His sketching skill and sailing know-how had earned him the job; the only drawback was that he had never seen the Bahama Islands, a drawback that we would correct during the next twenty-five years of producing the Guide.

But, back to these pumps. Harry decided that sailing with the various mail boat captains throughout the Out Islands would be the quickest way for him to learn the Bahamian waters, thus our trip to the Abacos. One of Nassau's saltiest seadogs, Steve, had agreed to deliver us to the *Stede Bonnet* and introduce us to his old buddy, Captain Archie Bethel. And it was Steve who had just admonished us to listen for the pumps. Being new to boats, (the cruise to Spanish Wells was the first, with the exception of a transatlantic trip during my junior year in college) I could not distinguish between the sounds of the engines and these mysterious pumps. But, as Harry did not seem concerned, I stayed silent, assuming he would explain it once we were aboard.

As I recall, the 85-mile run up the North East Providence Channel was a smooth one of about ten hours. However, the seas were the least of my problems on our first night aboard a Bahamian Out Island "mail", as those venerable old ladies were called back then. After a simple supper of fish and an odd, gluey substance called grits, we sat on deck for hours watching the myriad of stars and listening to the hiss of the waves, a perfect honeymoon setting.

Filled with wellbeing we retired to our "first class cabin" (the difference between first and second class being that first class bunks had mattresses), climbed into our tiny bunks and turned out the bare light bulb hanging from the overhead. I don't remember my thoughts, but they were undoubtedly something terribly romantic, and then – the first unidentified object brushed my face. Thinking it was a moth; I flicked it away. There came a second and a third, and then a rush of wings and feet – feet? What type of moth has feet? With a shriek I leapt out of my bunk and bumped into Harry, who was springing from his bunk. On went the lights; and we had our first introduction to Bahamian cockroaches. YUUK! To this day they give me the creeps. We spent the rest of the night sitting out on deck, vowing to buy a can of Raid at our first Abaco grocery store.

Dawn brought a spectacular sunrise and the unusual rock formation of Hole in the Wall on the southern coast of Great Abaco. Cockroaches and pumps forgotten (I don't believe they stopped during the night) we watched as Captain Bethel guided us into the huge bay at Cherokee settlement where the offloading of freight began. It was a tedious project, as when the tide is down as it was that morning, the crew had to wade, pushing the tender ahead of them, the last one hundred feet to the end of Cherokee's 300´ dock. It seemed to us that a dredge would solve Cherokee's problem, but here it is some forty years later, and at low tide you still have to walk the last one hundred feet to Cherokee's dock.

Freight and passengers safely ashore, we steamed up and in North Bar Channel, around Witch Point and anchored off East Side to let the Marsh Harbour passengers disembark. Sometime during this part of the voyage, Captain Bethel called us into the wheel house and asked/told me that since the cook had jumped ship in Cherokee (to be with his new bride) and since I was the only female aboard, I would be doing the cooking until he could find another cook. I did not accept this request/order very eagerly as, with the exception of salads and popcorn, I had just started cooking a few months ago. Poor Harry, poor crew and poor me.

But, determined to be a good sport, I went down to the galley to whip up some tuna salad sandwiches for lunch. After all, every boat has a store of canned goods, right? Wrong. This boat had a large block of lard, dry grits, hard bread, canned bully beef and a few onions. Obviously, the Captain planned on stopping at the first grocery store along the way. Don't laugh; back then I still thought that all settlements had grocery stores and snack bars and perhaps even a Laundromat and shower. Yes, I did have a lot to learn.

The following days were a blur of breathtakingly beautiful passages over fabled "gin-clear" water. Nights were spent moving from the insect-free deck to the relative comfort of our bunks (as a thorough scrubbing with Blanco Bleach, an Out Island staple, had killed off most of our night visitors) and the visits to tiny settlements, the likes of which Harry and I had never imagined. I won't elaborate on the meals.

And then came Green Turtle Cay. Our one other first class cabin passenger hailed from Green Turtle and assured me that there was a real hotel there with rooms and good food. I couldn't wait. Quickly leaving Harry on the dock to chat with the local skippers, I ran up the narrow cement road to the New Plymouth Inn with visions of a hot bath and fresh vegetables dancing in my head. I guess it never occurred to me to look into a mirror before entering those sacred walls. The spotlessly attired English gentlewoman took one look at me and announced that she "did not take passengers from the mail" before shutting the screen door in my face.

Back to my floating home I went, still dirty, hot and angry. Harry thought it all fairly amusing and said, "Well, there's always Hope Town."

"Ha," thought I, "I do not intend to be insulted twice in one trip."

But by the time we reached Hope Town late the next day, my optimism had returned and my desire for a bath outdid my reluctance to be turned away a second time.

Catching a ride in with the first tender load of freight, as we had no passengers for Hope Town, I barely glanced at the majestic, red and white striped lighthouse on the west side of the harbor. I just went straight to the stone steps leading up to a tall building at the east end of the harbor. It was a hot morning; the steps were steep, and I was slowing down as I reached the wide, stone landing, when I heard an angel's voice asking, "Good Lord, who are you and where did you come from?"

When she had heard my answers she led me inside to a cool, comfortable living room, brought me an iced, yes **iced**, tea and later took me to her own bathroom, turned on the hot water and left me alone for what seemed like a blissful eternity.

That evening, Harry and I joined her and her husband, Marcel, for the first of many memorable meals that she would make for us over the ensuing years.

The angel was Ruth Maury of the Hope Town Harbour Lodge and little did I know then that twenty-five years later I would move to Hope Town permanently and eventually marry her brother. But that is another story with many cruises, cooking lessons and Out Island friends in between.

The pumps? Oh yes, the pumps. What our friend Steve was referring to were the *Stede Bonnet's* three bilge pumps that ran continuously due to her many leaks. And to the best of my knowledge they never did stop running until the day that old mail was lost in Hurricane Betsy.

SO YOU'RE THINKING OF COMING TO HOPE TOWN
Steve Best

So you're thinking of coming to Hope Town? Allow me to offer a few observations not provided in the travel brochures. My views are entirely subjective, so you may want to get a second opinion. You will find this quite easy, because everyone here has an opinion, and most are willing to share.

Hope Town is the principal settlement on Elbow Cay, somewhat larger than a crossroad, and substantially smaller than a metropolis. If you are visiting for the first time, you will doubtless fit into one of three categories.

Category No. 1 is comprised of those who will never come back. This includes those who don't like animals and similar critters, and most people who have Type A personalities even on vacation. If you fit either description, I suggest you avoid the Family Islands altogether, and book a room at the Atlantis on Paradise Island. It won't hurt our feelings because we're already getting too many people who fit into Category No. 3.

With respect to animals, most rental cottages come with a cat, although this particular amenity is seldom advertised. If you are sunning on the beach, you may be startled by the touch of a dog's wet nose on your back. Very likely, it could be one of my dogs. This is part of our sophisticated anti-terrorist system. The dog is looking for weapons of mass destruction and sometimes just an affectionate pat. You may hear frogs croaking in cisterns at night. You may find lizards or hermit crabs walking around your bedroom. To us they are welcome scavengers, as they feed on spiders and other unmentionable insects. Oh yes, there are those, too. Rumor has it they were here before we were and will be here when we're gone. A bird may fly into your house if you leave the windows or doors open. Getting them out will test your ingenuity, but it is far preferable to keeping everything shut.

If you don't like sand or sea air, you might try the Great Smoky Mountains instead of the Bahamas. No matter what you do, sand and salt find a way into a house, along with the rust that seems to appear overnight. If you don't like returning greetings, bring a set of blinders. If you insist on immediate service, bring some peanut butter and jelly or whatever else you eat at home. If you can't live without electricity twenty-four hours a day, get a house with a generator, and if the sound of a generator drives you batty, as it does me, see the above advice for animal haters.

I will now move on to Category No. 2, which includes those of you who will return occasionally. This is the largest of the categories. If you like your oceans with spectacular colors, your beaches pristine and uncrowded, a multitude of islands, restaurants and bars to visit, and if you have a Type B personality when on vacation, you will fit comfortably into Category No. 2 and will be eligible to join Category No. 3 at any time. I write this article primarily for you, because those in Category No. 1 will be uninterested, and those in No. 3 already know the magic that is Hope Town.

Category No. 3 has all those who return to Hope Town every year or every chance they get. So what makes this place so special?

First, I will tell you a little about Hope Town. How could you plan a village any better? It has a financial district, located at the north end of the settlement, consisting of an international bank open from 10 a.m. (approximately) until 2 p.m. every Tuesday. Once a week is fine as there isn't that much to spend money on. It has a hotel district, located at the south end of the settlement, consisting of the Hope Town Harbour Lodge. Its restaurant district is sprinkled throughout the settlement, on both sides of the harbor, and numbers five within the city limits, and several more nearby. There is a public disposal system unmatched by almost every city in the world, collecting trash three times a week, including trash from boats. Its transportation system runs on time, and consists of Albury's Ferry, with six daily visits to and from Marsh Harbour, plus twenty-four hour charter service. There is no bus system, but you can get from one end of the village to the other in a period from ten minutes to two hours, depending upon how many friends you meet along the way. Other conveyances are prohibited, except bicycles and skateboards, unless you are a necessary commercial vehicle or have a disability. Hope Town does experience occasional gridlock, as there is room for only one vehicle to pass, but it doesn't last long, and there is no road rage.

Two markets provide an amazing variety of foods. One even has a modern scanning checkout system, but this has had precious little effect on checkout time, since customers still like to chat with the checker-outers. One of these checker-outers has a new baby available for viewing, which more than offsets the efficiency of high technology. Remember, when shopping for groceries, no one in Hope Town is in a hurry, so buy your ice cream last. And be sure to get a loaf of Vernon's bread.

Hope Town has a very good library, reflecting the personality of its inhabitants who contribute the books and serve as volunteer librarians. The books and the inhabitants range from nautical to naughty. We are still waiting for Mr. Dewey or one of his descendants to arrive with their decimal system, not to mention modems, but until then we manage to keep track of the books quite nicely.

There is a museum, again manned (and womanned) by volunteers. We don't frisk or otherwise violate you when you enter or leave, although I cannot vouch for the discretion of each and every docent.

If your house doesn't come with a cat, don't fret. Right next to the Harbour

View Grocery is a house once occupied by the late, lamented Lilly, where you can borrow one and honor her memory. Tell me one other place that offers this service.

Hope Town even has a floating lottery. None of the proceeds goes to the government, but benefits only local projects. Sherluck is more than willing to sell you any number of raffle tickets and you needn't seek him out. Eventually he will find you.

There is a reliable fire department, with one truck in the village and one in White Sound, the second-largest and only other settlement on Elbow Cay. Neither of the trucks has a hook-and-ladder because the only structure which might need one is the lighthouse, and it is unreachable by road and is basically nonflammable... except for one small kerosene lantern that you can blow out easier than the candles on a birthday cake for a two-year old child.

Hope Town has a constable of sorts, and once had a policeman and may yet again. In the meantime, just behave yourself. I seldom carry money, so I have little fear of being mugged. I don't feel the need to live in a gated community, or even a house I can lock. The humidity has caused my doors to swell so I can't even close them completely. One of these days I may get around to planing them down, but I will still not lock them because the only person I'll probably lock out is myself. Instead, I've decided not to live anywhere that I feel the need to lock my door. Anyhow, I'm guarded constantly by two ferocious Jack Russell terriers who most likely would lick any thief to death.

There is also life outside of Hope Town. Geographically, the settlement is but a small part of Elbow Cay, which is more than five miles long and as much as a half mile wide. Contrary to local lore, Elbow Cay was not named by people who drank a lot, but for its shape. Like most islands, it has a South End and a North End, both of which are bordered by water, which is probably their only common characteristic. The people to the north seem to come from everywhere, while people from the South End seem to come from Coral Cables or Boca Raton. Economically, people living at the North End range from wealthy to comfortable, but you can't tell which is which and no one really cares. Opulent houses don't exist in the North End. Perhaps it's a sort of reverse peer pressure; perhaps it's because people are happier outside. Most people there are separated from Hope Town by about a mile of very bumpy road, but are villagers in every other sense of the word.

This description also applies to some people on the South End, which is about four miles distant, but most inhabitants seem two hundred miles away in spirit. The South End is blessed by cool ocean breezes most of the year; ceiling fans substitute quite nicely when days are still. But, like most Floridians, people there prefer artificially cooled houses where their expensive furnishings are protected from ravages of salty sea air. The South End does not have reefs to lessen the corrosive effects of nasty weather, which may explain why houses there seem to turn over much faster than elsewhere. But maybe it's because its inhabitants are not into the rhythm of life so special to Hope Town and most of Elbow Cay. For them Hope Town is a nice place to visit, but they wouldn't want to live there. Something like New York City, but with less traffic and better trash service.

What is this rhythm? Everyone seems to agree that it revolves around the people, who include the locals, who chose to stay here and the foreigners who chose to live here.

Economically, the foreigners range from rich to quite modest, but the rich try not to show it. Some second homes are powerboats and sail boats. Politically, some foreigners are conservative, some are liberal, and some aren't interested. All are self-reliant, at least to some extent. You cannot call special services to have someone come replace a light bulb.

They are young, middle-aged and old, but a common characteristic of the old ones (of which I guess I am one) is that they don't seem old, or act old, and don't want to spend the rest of their lives just around other old people who talk old. To date no one has expressed interest in hearing about my medical history. Everyone seems to like each other, and if they don't, they keep it a secret.

That still doesn't explain the rhythm that brought us all together. Here is one important factor. Several years ago an urban planner who lived in Charleston, South Carolina, talked of places that had harmony and those that did not. She felt that Hope Town had a visual harmony unequalled almost anywhere. With its natural harbor and unplanned but tasteful development, and its small size, it had a scale that makes people feel comfortable. I agree. I never tire of walking through the settlement, and I still experience a thrill upon seeing the lighthouse in the distance when I return and head for Hope Town once more. For all those who make it their first home or their second home, there is no substitute, and this is a common bond.

That doesn't explain it all, but it's enough for me. A part of life's treasure is its mystery, so I will just treasure Hope Town, rather than try to solve that mystery.

April 2003

HOW WE FOUND HOPE TOWN
Tony and Elaine Bennett

I believe in fate, God has a plan for us;
all we must do is have faith enough to follow his plan.

Tony and I would sit on the deck of our cottage at Wise Island and wonder if there was a place on earth as beautiful as the Pacific North West. It is so peaceful and quiet; all that disturbed our thoughts were the beating of the gulls' wings as they swooped and dove to retrieve their supper of star fish and the water lapping against the rocks under the deck. Sitting there, watching the fireball of yet another beautiful sunset paint the clouds and outline the hills across the water, we would dream of this other magical island where we could go when the cool, dark, dreary days of winter descended on our tranquil beautiful little piece of paradise.

Every February I would declare that I was allergic to winter and must be taken away to see the sun. We had lived in Hawaii, visited many lovely places including Costa Rica and Puerto Rico and many other Caribbean islands but had never been tempted to pull up roots and move. However, flying back from Puerto Rico as we looked out of the airplane window, we spied beautiful islands, surrounded by turquoise water and ribbons of white sandy beaches. The Bahamas. They seemed to be beckoning us; fate had taken another turn in our lives.

That following summer we read all the travel books we could find on the Bahamas but nothing really jumped out and grabbed us. Perhaps this time, it wasn't meant to be. Nassau and Freeport did not seem to be our "cup of tea." Then Tony came home with a copy of *Cruising World.*

"Elaine, I think I have found the place for us. Look at this ad."

I read the ad carefully and it said this cottage was on an island, not serviced by ferries, no electricity, a place for the adventuresome.

"Sounds very much like Wise Island doesn't it?" remarked Tony excitedly. He contacted the owner of the cottage who tried to explain that this was not the vacation for the faint of heart. Tony confidently told Larry that we had a cottage on a similar island in the Pacific Northwest and we knew all about living without the trappings of a modern world! So, after sending many letters and video of our island and cottage, Larry agreed that perhaps we were suitable for being allowed to enjoy his piece of paradise, Lubbers Quarters.

God has a funny way of making sure you go through the hoops before he allows you to realize how fortunate you are. I had just been accepted as a mature student to follow my dream of being a teacher. Tony had decided he did not want to stay in the government organization he was working for and wanted to branch out into the different life of a consultant. I, being the cautious one, decided we could not afford a holiday this year and perhaps should put this idea on hold for a year or two. No, we need a holiday to regroup and think about what we are going to do; we are going! Tony booked the tickets and we set off on yet another adventure on February 14, 1991.

As we settled down in our seats in the plane, Tony gave me a lovely card with a pretty gold necklace in it. This, I thought, must be the start of something wonderful. So, I settled down and drifted off to sleep dreaming of the wonderful adventure I was about to embark on.

We arrived in steamy Miami and were directed to our little plane sitting out on the hot tarmac. After the stewardess had rearranged the seating several times, moving various people to various seats and checking the weight of bags etc., we were informed that this was necessary due to not being able to refuel in Marsh Harbour. Finally, she seemed satisfied with the seating arrangement, everyone sitting towards the front of the plane; I presumed that the baggage was loaded towards the back of the plane, plus all the hand luggage they had stuffed into the wings. We lumbered down the runway and finally took off.

Where was that turquoise water I remembered? All I could see were white caps. The plane was buffeted about by the winds and we bounced across over angry looking water. Finally, we were informed to make sure our seat belts were in place and our seats upright as we were about to land in Marsh Harbour. The runway looked awfully short and the sight of a plane wreck didn't make me feel very confident. The winds were tossing us as we bumped down the runway to a grinding halt in front of a small building. We had arrived in Marsh Harbour.

We passed through customs with no problems and found a taxi to take us to the Conch Inn where we would spend our first night. We were shown our room, one with a view of the angry grey water. Oh well, let's go for a walk. As we got tossed along the road, we realized the temperature was cooler than when we left Victoria; there was something terribly wrong with this picture. Marsh Harbour really didn't seem to have any endearing qualities about it so we decided to go back and turn in for the night. The wind howled all night and the sound of the water crashing outside our window, please don't let the window break I thought as I tossed and turned trying desperately to think of that beautiful turquoise water I had envisioned. After a very restless night we went down to the restaurant for breakfast, all the servers were dressed in parkas. We decided to make the best of it and ordered what they said was a specialty, chicken souse. When our breakfast arrived, I looked at Tony and he looked at me, broken chicken bones floating around in hot greasy water? Guess we won't order that again, little did we know at that time we would become very fond of chicken souse.

After breakfast, we called the ferry that was to take us to Parrot Cay to pick up our rental boat. "Surely, you are not sailing today in this weather? The sea is rough and we will not be able to go to Parrot Cay but we will "carry" you to Hope Town."

We were to be met by Jeff Gale. Fine, the ferry seemed quite sturdy and there were plenty of life jackets. "I wonder if they are used often?" I thought quietly to myself.

We were put off at the Lower Dock where we looked around to see if this mystical Jeff would appear. Would he be able to recognize us?

Suddenly, a pleasant young man with a broad smile introduced himself and told us he was taking us out to Parrot Cay to get our rental boat. His boat looked quite seaworthy but it wasn't anything as large as the ferry and they couldn't make it to Parrot Cay. What were our chances in this smaller boat? Jeff loaded us in and took off towards a small speck that he said was Parrot Cay. Once we got on land again I thought maybe we should change plans and perhaps we could rent the boat storage locker or something to stay in. Instead, Jeff showed us our rental boat; I thought his boat had had a baby — Oh Lord, this trip has been a big mistake.

He pointed out over the angry water to a thin line that he said was Lubbers Quarters, our destination. Jeff then informed us that we couldn't make it to the dock of the cottage we had rented because the seas were too rough. "Big surprise," I thought. We were directed to the other side of the island where the caretaker's cottage was and she would take us across the island on foot to our cottage for the adventuresome.

Thank heavens Tony was a former naval officer; I have confidence, he will find his way and won't drown us. We bundled our supplies and gear into black garbage bags, put on our wet weather gear and headed off.

The spray was splashing over us, we were soaking wet, but the good news was the water was warm. Finally, we arrived at the caretaker's cottage and tied up to her dock, Bahamian style with the stern out and the bow just touching the dock as we had been instructed. "Why can't they just tie up alongside like normal people and then perhaps you would get a chance of getting off safely?" Tony managed to toss the luggage and me up onto the dock without any terrible incident.

We raced down the dock towards the caretaker's cottage, but try as we might, we could not find any sign of life. We found out later she had left the island suddenly. Well, we have no other choice but to either stay here, or try and find the cottage ourselves. The island isn't that big, we will just take a quick walk across, find the cottage and come back for the rest of our stuff.

So, we put our backpacks on, and trudged across to a sandy beach, no sign of a cottage. "We must have taken the wrong path, we will go back and try again," said Tony. Next path led us to a plastic shack. "Oh no," I thought, "we really have done it this time. Adventuresome is hardly the word for this!" Then I noticed there was a dog tied up outside, surely the owner wouldn't have left the dog or was this part of the package, a guard dog? No, Elaine, come to your senses, this is not the cottage.

We retraced our steps yet again. The third try led us to a lovely house with smoke coming out of the chimney. I thought we had come to somewhere warm, a fireplace? The lady of the house was very kind and invited us in, informed us the caretaker was not on the island and pointed to the cottage we had rented. She was about to invite us to come in and warm ourselves by her lovely fire, when her unfriendly husband arrived and we realized he was not a warm and caring person. So, we thanked her for her trouble and trudged off towards our holiday-in-the-sun cottage.

It had only taken us three hours to find the cottage but we were so happy that we just collapsed and sat down to survey our surroundings.

"Tony, look. There are neighbours."

Being the chatty one, I rushed off to talk to them but they were not interested in hearing about my adventures; they had more important things on their minds, securing their boat and trying to prepare for the cold night ahead. So, I retreated to our cottage and started looking for blankets to put on the bed. I looked longingly out the window at the small spiral of smoke coming out of the cottage we had visited and wished I were back on Wise Island in front of my own lovely fire. We really had made the biggest mistake of our lives this time. I heated up a bowl of soup for us for supper and then we snuggled down, under a pile of blankets, looking at the mosquito net wondering why on earth they had a mosquito net in this god-forsaken place.

The next morning we awoke to a beautiful, warm, sunny day. The doves were cooing, the winds gently blowing and the sky was a beautiful shade of blue. Tony said, "Why don't we take a run into Hope Town and go to the Lodge for their Sunday brunch, then you won't have to think about cooking today. We can just enjoy the moment."

Great idea, off we trekked across the island. How did it take us so long yesterday to find our way? This walk was so lovely and pleasant across this pretty little island. We got into our 13' Boston Whaler and headed across the turquoise water to Hope Town. Looking over the side of the boat I spied various sea urchins, starfish and then, out in front of the boat a pair of dolphins leaped out of the water. I glanced up at the sky and the clouds had taken on a beautiful turquoise colour reflecting the water below. We breathed in the beauty all around us and enjoyed our run into the harbour, with all the beautiful little homes along the waterfront, the majestic red and white lighthouse standing guard over this little piece of paradise.

We got out of the boat, making sure we tied up as Jeff had instructed us. Now it made perfect sense to tie up with the stern out, more room for more boats. As it was still early, we ambled through the settlement at a loss for words; both of us were deep in our own thoughts. We wandered up to the top of the dune to gaze out at the ocean lapping the beautiful miles of white sandy beach. We had truly found somewhere very special.

Just then, the church bells chimed out and as I turned to look at Tony.

"Elaine, I think we have found what we have been looking for?"

"Yes, and that is the house I want to live in down there: Green Shutters."

"But it isn't even for sale Elaine!"

How we came to live in Green Shutters is another story!

Vacation in Hope Town
Irv Gubitz

"Gracious, what are you doing," she screamed as she opened the door. She was loaded with parcels from shopping at Vernon's Store. Cupboards and closets opened, dishes and clothes just strewn. Furniture moved, curtains torn down, and the place practically in ruin.

She realized something was terribly wrong and tonight there would be no cooking.

"What's happening? Why are you doing this, and for what are you possibly looking?"

Her husband rolled up the carpets and turned over a chair, mumbled to himself as he started to swear. She shouted for him to stop and smashed a pan on the sink. He froze and stared at her, hesitated and reached for a drink.

"This is incredible, what's going on? Why are you destroying this place?"

He replied, "I can't understand it, I never expected this terrifying pace."

"What are you talking about, what do you mean? The holiday has been so sublime."

"You're right, but five weeks have already gone and I'm looking where the hell they put the time."

(He's a silly chap but his mind is not so slow
Since for each of us the good times come and go.
Who can ever fathom why
The time in Hope Town seems to fly!!)

VISITING MARSH HARBOUR
Steve Best

People in Hope Town occasionally go to Marsh Harbour to shop for necessities. Marsh Harbour is the economic hub of the Abacos, a group of islands in the Bahamas. Recently a friend told me that she took the ferry over in the morning and returned early in the afternoon. When she got home she prepared a dinner that her husband could warm up later and she went to bed for the rest of the day. I know the feeling.

People living in Hope Town are normally active and energetic, and fill each day with endless activity of some sort. But walk around Marsh Harbour for a couple hours, even with time off for a pleasant lunch at Wally's, and it's time to crash. For many tourists, shopping is the drug of choice, and one morning in Hope Town exhausts all the possibilities there. Other islands have much the same offerings. Each bar has its own tee shirts, but that's about all.

So some people decide to take a day trip to Marsh Harbour for pleasure shopping, because that sounds like the biggest mall. Forget it, unless your idea of fun at home is going to Costco or Target. If that's the case, you'll probably find the same items back there, only much cheaper. The best bargain is still rum.

Here are a few words about Marsh Harbour for the uninitiated. If New York City is the Big Apple, Marsh Harbour is the Big Cumquat. (Some might say prune pit, but prunes aren't indigenous to the Bahamas; then again, I've never seen an apple orchard in New York.) Geographically, Marsh Harbour is the size of midtown Manhattan. It has about the same number of people as a tenement house in South Bronx.

Marsh Harbour has a ferry system that beats the commuter train system in the Big Apple hands down. The Albury ferries are clean and they run on time. Albury is English for Mussolini. Marsh Harbour has more taxis per capita, and all the drivers speak English. This doesn't mean, necessarily, that you will understand them, but if you live more than fifty miles from New York, you will understand them better than any cab driver in the Big Apple. Here are a few tips: If a word begins with an "h," the Bahamian drops the "h" and stores it in his brain for later use; when he comes to a word beginning with a vowel, he then adds the "h" back in. For example, the ferry leaves Marsh 'Arbour, not Marsh Harbour, and it arrives, not in Hope Town, but in 'Ope Town, and the driver has saved two "h's" that he can use that hevening when he greets his wife, Heleanor. If you listen carefully, you can hear a double switch in a single word. Hanyow, that's what they tell me.

Years ago my neighbor, Harriet Jones, told me of the time her gas line seemed to be clogged. Willard, the local gas man inspected and informed her, "Miss 'arriet, your problem is that you have hair in your horifices." Harriet said she blushed, and if she hadn't known his dialect, she would have slapped his face.

If a word begins with a "v," a "w" is substituted. Recently I overheard a Bahamian giving directions to a German tourist. "When you come to the wee in the willage, go left," said the Bahamian.

"Vhat's a wee in the willage?" responded the German. As he walked away, the Bahamian remarked to his friend, "'e sounds like the willage hidiot."

Although Marsh Harbour has a movie theatre and holds a carnival every few years, the Big Apple is still slightly ahead of the Big Cumquat culturally. And it has more skyscrapers. Marsh Harbour's only skyscrapers are its radio towers. In fact, a third floor in Marsh Harbour is called a penthouse.

Neither place is big on supermarkets. The Golden Harvest burned down about a year ago, and they say they are going to rebuild it, but all I've seen so far is a sign promising a modern, enlarged supermarket. Marsh Harbour needs prime commercial property for storing its old trailers, boats and similar items, and last year a huge liquor store went up on the property across the street, forcing them all to move to the Golden Harvest lot. I think there's a better chance that Osama Bin Laden will become a born-again Christian than we see another Golden Harvest. That's too bad. Last year Hope Town residents saved almost a thousand dollars by buying groceries in Marsh Harbour instead of Hope Town, and it cost them little more than ten thousand dollars in fuel, ferries, and taxis to do so.

A word of caution: during the summer it rains more often in Marsh Harbour than anywhere else in the world except a rain forest. If you bring an umbrella, it might not rain; but if you don't, it most certainly will. An inflatable raft or life jacket is also recommended. Not so much for the ride over, but for when you get there. Marsh Harbour has no sewer system, and smaller people can get swept all the way to Dundas Town.

Marsh Harbour is the only place I know where you can buy conch salad at the gasoline station. Sometimes it produces more heat than gasoline and its cheaper, but you should probably not put it in your tank. If the gasoline station is out of conch salad, try the hardware store. It also has good pastries.

If you see a store locked, and the sign on the door says something like "back in an hour," don't count on it. Except on ferries, the Bahamian hour is a minimum of sixty-five minutes long, and the average is well over a hundred. Incidentally, the Bahamian does pronounce the "h" in hour, but that's only because nobody else does. The Bahamians are wery independent.

If you're crazy enough to buy or rent a car, please remember that in the Bahamas you drive in the middle, unless its already taken, and then you move to the left. If you insist on moving to the right, I suggest you trade for a front-end loader.

Come to think of it, the Big Cumquat is not much different from the almost extinct American small town. It's friendly, and most people try to help you find what you're looking for. There's no Walmart, no Home Depot, no McDonald's, but you can find almost everything you're looking for, unless they're out of it. But you can probably get along fine without it until it comes in. You can always find a beautiful beach, magnificent water, and good company. Just be ready for a nap when you get back to Hope Town.

SHED ON THE BEACH BEHIND ALBURY HOUSE
Eleanor Epler

Our unpainted shed
A survivor
A site of stories
The old houses in Hope Town settlement have stood
Through gales, rains, the hurricanes
Sited in the safe spots on the cays

The shed is a symbol to me
Of strength and stubbornness
It may pre-date our famous lighthouse
Recently, our owner, here in the settlement,
Was requested to have it torn down
Because it is unsightly
A visual blight.

I say, preserve some structure from the past
The unpainted wood attests to a by-gone time
When effort and money had to go to basic survival
Rather than decorative enhancements
Now a painter's focus, our shed is bulwark against
The wind and weather

Our shed proclaims independence
Individuality,
Hope Town identity.

HAPPY HOUR AT CAPTAIN JACK'S
Mary Balzac

Empty bar stools filling one by one
And booths by bar as locals call for beer,
Wine and rum, even coffee and decaf iced tea.
Relaxing work weary bones and brains
Catchin' up on latest news, mostly local,
And events. Roads? Docks? BatelCo and BEC
Catchin' fish? No grouper this month, please.

Who's walkin' in with whom?
Amy and Dave, both last named Pierce,
Not related that I know
Seat opposite in a booth. Amy talks
Of new grandbaby and Turtle Hill
Dave *aka* The Governor or Ancient Mariner
Shares a story from his years at sea.

Mary meets Perry Tuesday's at four
They take a table on the deck. Perry, coffee
Or white wine. Mary, once a week Goombay
Smash. Lois (pronounced Loyce) never forgets
To tell Althea to make it weak. Philosophizing
And buddist talk. Any good books?
How goes the carving and selling of same?

Roger, 'round the world sailor, a French man
Through and through. "Ah zee Americans"
Making a face and lifting a hand as
Only a Frenchman can do.... Then
Smiling wide with pleasantness
Toward this American sitting and sharing
In a threesome on the deck.

Don and Welly, Dan, Sara and Deanna, sit on stools.
Shane tends tables now. Lois gone home.
Althea's done her daily round, Mike takes over,
Or Neil when home from Embry Riddle.
Peanuts out in coffee cups on tables and bar.
Lana passing fish nantua or fried squash rounds
Talks with all and laughs, a happy sound.

Rubber dinghies to the dock. Live aboards
Climb ladders, head toward inside gathering
Laughter reigns with smiles and local jokes
Poking gentle fun with one another
Part timers come up from south by boat
Bike and golf cart from the north. Tourists slip
Between stools and booths toward outside tables.

Abacays heads out the harbor toward Man O' War
Albury's Ferry arrives on its last daily run
Sun sets below peach, pale yellow, and violet clouds
Framing Hope Town's red and white striped claim to fame.
A flicker, just visible, signals the lighting of the
Kerosene mantle which the lighthouse
Keeper will tend throughout the night.

January 2004

WARNING
Shelley Boyd Malone

March to March
200 years of winds have whistled through the village
This wind blows in
Crowding the ferry
Five bags a person deep
Plumbago and yellow oleander reach out
In an attempt to hide
Plastic trellises where wood
Once rotted gracefully in the salt air
Miss Lillie's cats wait
Curled on the porch where three silk roses honor her
Shuttered door
Hammers pound the air of a pavilion where
Perry's small studio once gently sloped
Franklin and Douglas have bad days now
Seeking wellness in Marsh Harbour
Nicki and Miracle still walk Will through the lanes
That will one day house only visitors
Seeking the sun and a rum or two
In the Bahamian brochured "quaintness" of Hope Town

Sounds will change
Your children's children will not remember
The lovely lilt of the h'Abaconian accent calling from a porch
TV will put a pillow over that soft sweetness
Air conditioners quiet neighbors you will never know
Porches will be replaced by pools no one uses

You will wait for rain that doesn't come
Because there is little green left
You will mourn the loss of termite-eaten wood
With its imperfect edges and
The familiar voices of your ancestry adding (h)'atches where they aren't
Taking them from the (H)ope Town you once knew
Your island will become a stranger to you

I am from Key West
I know these things

March 2002

CHANGES
Audrey Malone

Casuarinas whisper in the breeze
Towering over silent tombstones
Broken, neglected
Marking the graves
Of loved ones long ago passed away
Pine needles fall gently
Softly enfolding them
In a blanket of silence
These are long forgotten
Does anyone remember or care
That the resting places
Of our ancestors
Who brought us here?
Are fading away
Lost in what we call progress

March 2002

ELBOW REEF LIGHTSTATION

THREE LOVES – WITH A LATITUDE ADJUSTMENT
Maureen Miller

Two of my three loves have stood silently, for several centuries now, in approximately the same longitude. With a latitude adjustment of twelve degrees, one comforts me in summer, the other in winter.

Two beacons, built as navigation aids. One lives totally as in the past, true to its history while the other guards its past only in structure. Its internal parts have been updated with modern technology.

One of these beacons stands in the Chesapeake Bay, just at the mouth of the South River. At latitude 38.54 N and longitude 76.26 W, its official name is the Thomas Point Shoal Lighthouse, but everyone calls it the Thomas Point Lighthouse. This historical marker I first met when I came to the Bay area in the 90s. Now it is more than just a marker—for, as I ply the Chesapeake waters in the summer, it is a waypoint, a reference, an indication that I am nearing home.

The second beacon stands on the west side of Hope Town Harbour, on Elbow Cay in the Bahamas. At latitude 26.32 N and longitude 76.58 W, it is officially named the Elbow Reef Lightstation. However, it's much better known as the Hope Town Lighthouse. My introduction to this lighthouse was as a 'must see' tourist stop when I first visited the Bahamas last year. Today, it plays a prominent part in my life, as it greets me each morning as I step into my winter office and lulls me to sleep each evening with it's bright flashes.

The physical presence of my two loves differ. The squat Thomas Point structure, set on pilings, rises a mere forty-three feet above the Bay's mean high waters. Just south of the historic city of Annapolis, it warns those who ply the Chesapeake of the dangerous shoal on which it stands. In contrast, the red-and-white, candy-striped Hope Town structure soars a majestic one hundred and twenty feet. It warns seafarers of the dangerous reefs in the Atlantic to the east of Elbow Cay. And while the lighthouse at Thomas Point was built to hold the lighthouse lantern and mechanism as well as its keepers, their garden, sheep and cattle, entirely within, the Hope Town lighthouse contains only the lantern and mechanism. Its lighthouse keepers and their victuals are housed in separate buildings.

But the birthdates, lives and souls of these two are similar. Both were born in the 19th century and continue, to today, to ply their trade as in the past. The lighthouse at Thomas Point is the only screwpile, cottage-type lighthouse still standing at its original site in the Chesapeake Bay. The Hope Town lighthouse is one of the last three hand-wound, kerosene-burning lighthouses remaining in the world. Their beacons, also known as their souls, were originally lit by primitive whale oil with simple wicked devices. In time, these were upgraded to beautiful Fresnel lenses—lenses, developed by a French engineer in 1821, comprised of a series of crystal prisms that focused the light source into a powerful beam.

My love at Thomas Point was, until recently, outfitted by a fourth order lens - standing about two and one-half feet tall with an inside diameter of twenty inches. Today its 250mm solar-powered white ray is visible from thirteen miles and red flash from eleven miles.

The soul of my Hope Town love remains a first order Fresnel lens. Standing eight feet tall with an inside diameter of six feet, it pulses out its five white flashes every fifteen seconds, which are visible for fifteen nautical miles.

So they live, two mighty structures braving the elements. Elements that often first strike one—and then the other—as did Hurricane Floyd in 1999 and Isabel in 2003. But what a difference that twelve degrees in latitude makes. For as the lighthouse at Hope Town basks, as I do, in sunshine and warmth during the winter months, that at Thomas Point is contending with freezing winds and ice flows. In the summer, however, they are practically equals, beckoning boaters, photographers and tourists alike through warm, humid days with their brightly painted, picturesque structures, and keeping seafarers from dangerous shoals and reefs at night with their strong beacons.

Oh, yes, my third love? That would be my husband—really my first love— who joins me in my seasonal latitude adjustment and unabashedly uses my other two loves as models in his paintings.

March 2004

THE POLKA DOT LIGHTHOUSE
Steve Best

The following story is entirely fictitious. Any resemblance to lighthouses living or dead is purely coincidental.

"Benjamin! I want you and Harold to go out and sweep off the sidewalks, while I fix your breakfast."

"Yes Ma'am."

"Now!"

"Yes ma'am." When his mother called him Benjamin, Benjy knew she meant business. He picked up the push broom and dustpan and began to walk outside.

"C'mon Harold."

When Harold got outside he looked up and his eyes became like two sand dollars.

"Wow!" Benjy's cousin, Harold, had come to Hopeful Harbour from Crooked Island to spend the summer and he had paid little attention to the lighthouse that now stood beside him, as he had arrived after dark. Now he gaped at a series of red and white stripes reaching up almost to the clouds, and he was awestruck. Harold had never seen anything taller than a casuarina tree.

Benjy's father, Jaster, was the keeper of the Wishbone Cay Lighthouse, and Benjy was the youngest of his nine sons. Jaster always wanted enough sons for a basketball team, but habits are tough to break and number six arrived in due course. Jaster didn't want any of his kids riding the bench so he decided to go for a baseball team instead. He finally got his shortstop and named him Benjamin, hoping he, indeed, would be the lastborn, as in the Bible. Jaster's wife, Condaleeza, knew her Bible much better than he did, but she didn't have the heart to tell him that the Biblical Benjamin was the firstborn.

Benjy's parents soon learned he was a very special child and worth waiting for. All creatures took to him, and he to them. The first words he ever spoke were to a curly-tailed lizard that climbed up his stroller, sat in front of him and turned its head as if trying to understand what he was saying. When he walked past hermit crabs, they didn't escape into their shells, but followed him. Birds would land on his shoulder chirping, and he chirped right back. Jaster used to say jokingly, "I'll bet Benjy could get the lighthouse to talk."

As Harold stood gaping, his head seemingly stuck in the upward position, Benjy said casually, "That's my friend, the lighthouse. Good morning, lighthouse."

"Good Morning, Benjy."

Benjy looked up. "Who said that? It sounded like it came from up in the lighthouse."

"It did, Benjy, and you can call me Leticia."

Benjy put his hands on his hips, and shouted. "The lighthouse isn't open for visitors yet. You're not supposed to be up there, and if my dad sees you, you're going to be in trouble."

"I'm not up in the lighthouse, Benjy. I am the lighthouse."

Harold tugged at Benjy's shirt. "B...Benjy, I think I hear your mother calling. Let's go inside."

"No Harold, we have to sweep the sidewalk first."

Once again, a voice came from the lighthouse.

"Before you begin, Benjy, I have an itch on my wall just to the right of you. Would you mind scratching it?"

"No problem, Leticia." Benjy began pushing the broom back and forth along the wall.

"How's that feel?"

"A little higher, now a little to the left. Yes, right there. Oh; that feels divine. Thanks so much, Benjy."

"Any time. Leticia, if you can talk, where's your mouth?"

"See that window about six stripes up? That's also my mouth; and my eyes see in every direction." Benjy began sweeping the walk. "How did you know my name?"

"I remember when you were born. After all, it was little more than five years ago and I'm going on a hundred and fifty. We had the most magnificent sunset that day and I shone extra bright all night long."

Harold tugged at Benjy's shirt again. "I think someone's up there playing a trick on you. If she talks, ask her who else she's talked to."

"Leticia, if you're really a talking lighthouse, why haven't you talked to anyone before?"

"No one ever talked to me before. I didn't think anyone would want to talk with me, and frankly, it wasn't part of my job description."

"I like talking with you, Leticia, and I think it's you, even if Harold doesn't."

"Thank you, Benjy. Actually, as I recall, I have tried to talk to people before, but there's only one person before who seemed to hear me. I think one may need to have ESP."

"What's ESP?"

"Extra sensory perception. It means you can hear things, or sense things that most people can't."

"Why can't they?"

"Maybe they just don't have that special power, or don't want to hear what they can't understand, or maybe they're just afraid."

"Why should they be afraid?"

"Remember I said there was one person I talked with. It was years and years ago. He loved to party and carry on, so much that they nicknamed him "Hoorah." He would come over late at night and we would talk for hours. Jaster would just shake his head after he relit me, and go back inside his house. I don't know if Jaster could hear me or not, but if he did, he never let on."

"Whatever happened to Hoorah?"

"I don't know. I do know that Hoorah sometimes bragged to others that we talked together, and once he made the mistake of bragging to the Constable. The following Monday a boat came over from the big island, and two men in white jackets took Hoorah with them, and he never returned. I still miss him."

"We won't tell anyone we talk to you. Will we, Harold?"

"No sirree!" Just then Benjy's mother came out of the house.

"Is that all the sweeping you got done, boy?"

"Yes ma'am. I been giving Harold sweeping lessons because he's never swept before."

"That's right, Miss Condaleeza. We ain't got sidewalks at home," added Harold.

"Who you chilrun think you're foolin'? Benjy, sometime I think you got that 'tenshun deficit disorder. You think I should get you some pills from the clinic?"

"No ma'am. We'll finish up soon."

"All you been doin' is talkin'. And who's that Laytisha?" Benjy thought quickly.

"She's my pet chicken. She went up in the lighthouse, and we're trying to get her to come back down."

"Well, you go up and get that stupid chicken and tell her the next time she goes up there, she's our dinner. Then you finish the sidewalk."

"Yes ma'am. C'mon, Harold"

Benjy and Harold walked up the lighthouse steps and stood inside until Miss Condaleeza went back in her house. Benjy whispered, "Whew, that was close. I don't think we better talk anymore today, Leticia." The lighthouse didn't make a sound in reply.

From then on Benjy and Harold only talked with Leticia late in the day, after the lighthouse was closed to visitors and Benjy's mother was preparing dinner. Of course, once it got dark, Leticia had to work until dawn, and in the morning she was usually too tired to talk.

One day late in July. Leticia seemed bothered.

"I've been going around in circles all day, which should be my time to rest. I overheard Hurricane Harry say that they're automating two more lighthouses in the Bahamas, and they want to automate me."

"What's 'automate'," asked Benjy.

"And who's Hurricane Harry?" chimed in Harold.

"Right now my light comes from a candle which your father or his assistant lights every two hours and they want to stick a light bulb in me instead, so they won't need your father anymore. Hurricane Harry is the President of the Wishbone Cay Lighthouse Association. He knows that doing that would be like tearing my heart out. I'll be left alone, like a stuffed animal."

Benjy began to cry. "And what will happen to us? Do you think they'll stick a light bulb in us, or stuff us?"

"I doubt it, Benjy, but it does mean we wouldn't see each other, or talk together anymore. I've lost so many of my relatives already. We used to communicate, and now they're just rotating robots."

Benjy scratched his head. "No wonder Mama and Daddy have seemed so worried. Is there anything we can do?"

"Maybe not you, but Hurricane Harry didn't get his name for nothing. I think he'll stir up a storm and find a way to keep me alive and you and your family on Wishbone Cay. In the meantime, let's enjoy each day."

In just three days it would be Independence Day in the Bahamas. On Wishbone Cay there would be a commemoration ceremony, followed by parties everywhere, and fireworks after dark, set off on the lighthouse grounds. The featured celebrant would be the lighthouse herself, and a band would play such songs as "You Light Up My Life" and "Come On, Baby, Light My Fire." Hurricane Harry was hoping this would draw favorable attention to his Save the Lighthouse Campaign. The lighthouse had been given a fresh coat of paint, and in order to make her seem more personal, Hurricane Harry was conducting a Name the Lighthouse competition.

"You look so beautiful, Leticia," said Benjy.

Leticia beamed, even though she was not yet lit.

"Thanks Benjy. I feel almost like I do at Christmas, when they dress me from top to bottom in lights. I'm like a queen wearing her crown jewels. But..." Leticia stopped beaming.

"But what, Leticia? What's the matter?"

"Well, don't think I don't appreciate what people have done, but I've been dressed like this for about one hundred and fifty years, and even a queen likes to wear a new outfit once in awhile. As you know, the Bahamian colors are black, yellow, and blue, and wouldn't it be nice if, for Independence Day, I could have polka dots those colors over my red and white stripes. I would look so...patriotic."

"And so beautiful, too," added Benjy. "Let me and Harold think about that, and we'll get back to you."

"Oh, would you?" Leticia beamed once more.

It didn't take Benjy and Harold long to come up with a plan. His daddy kept those colors of paint in his shed. Everything else they needed was on his daddy's boat. The following night they set Benjy's alarm clock for midnight and awoke with no problem. It was the Assistant Keeper's turn to light Leticia, and when he went back in his house, they unlocked the lighthouse and went to the top.

Benjy tied a knot in a three hundred-foot line after threading it through a pulley. Then he secured a boatswain's chair to the knot and hung a bucket from the chair. After letting both ends of the line fall to the ground, Benjy fastened the pulley to the railing that circles the viewing porch. He poured some paint in the bucket, set the alarm for fifteen minutes before the time his daddy would come up to relight Leticia, and put some talcum powder on his hands so they wouldn't chafe while he held on to the rope. Finally, he climbed into the boatswain's chair holding a mop.

"Now, Harold, you go down and work the line. When I turn my flashlight on and off, you let me down slowly until I give you another flash. Then stop. If I flash twice, move me from side to side slowly so I can add more spots as the wall gets wider near the bottom. When I get to the bottom, we'll go back up and do it again with a different bucket of paint. When we've done all three, we'll move the pulley over a few feet and begin again. O.K.?"

"No problem. Benjy, are you sure you're only five years old? You're smarter than my daddy."

Benjy didn't answer. He was already looking to see where he would put the spots. He dipped the mop in the bucket as he began his descent. He was able to push the mop against the wall and push himself away until Harold moved him down or to the side.

At quarter of two, the alarm went off. Harold pulled Benjy up, and Benjy pulled up the line and waited quietly until his daddy relit Leticia and went back in his house. They finished just before the alarm went off again. They managed to get to the basement with all the gear just as the assistant keeper came in the door.

As soon as he reached the top, they went out quietly and returned to the house. They planned to move the gear out in the morning. They both took showers before going to bed in order to get off any paint. Benjy forgot to bring back his alarm clock, but he was sure they would wake up at dawn, as they were anxious to see their artwork.

They didn't awake until about eight o'clock when they heard the frightening sound of a loud engine getting ever closer. They sprang out of bed and went to the window. They saw the red and white stripes of a U. S. Coast Guard helicopter hovering over the lighthouse. Men began descending a rope on to the porch where they had been just hours earlier. Three of the men carried sub-machine guns. Two others wore orange suits with hoods, and carried black boxes. Other helicopters hovered nearby and they could see the reflection of gun barrels coming from one of them.

"Wow'" exclaimed Benjy, "I thought Daddy might get mad, but not this mad. We better hide under the house."

Just as they got under the house, they heard Condaleeza's voice. "Benjy! Harold! Come quickly. We have to evacuate."

"What's 'evacuate,' Harold?"

"I don't know, Benjy, but it sounds a lot like 'automate,' and that's not good. Let's stay here."

Benjy agreed. After being called several times more, they heard Condaleeza say, "they must have gone over earlier on the ferry. There's no one around."

Shortly thereafter the Coastguardsmen with the guns came out the door of the lighthouse and circled the lighthouse with yellow plastic tape and a barricade; then stood by. Later, the orange men came out on the porch at the top of the lighthouse, and began ascending into the helicopter.

"Hey, Benjy, they're stealing our paint and our gear. I'm telling your daddy."

"I don't think that's such a good idea, Harold. Let's wait awhile."

A few minutes later, another helicopter landed on the lawn just beside the lighthouse. On its side were the letters, CNN. People began emerging. Some had video cameras; others had reflectors or other equipment. Finally a man and a woman exited, and stood not thirty feet from where Benjy and Harold were hiding. The woman began putting makeup on the man. Then someone signaled, and the man began speaking into a handheld microphone.

"Good morning. This is Wolf Blitzed. I'm standing next to the Wishbone Cay Lighthouse, which overlooks the heretofore peaceful settlement of Hopeful Harbour. Ordinarily the loudest sound you'll hear in this quiet Bahamian community is the crowing of roosters. But the roosters seem to have been frightened away by the roar of helicopter rotors that have been hovering overhead. The United States and Bahamian Governments are investigating what may be an imminent terrorist attack in this unlikeliest of places.

"The Wishbone Cay lighthouse is one of the few remaining lighthouses in the world that is not automated and run by machines. For example, every one of the lighthouses in the United States is now automated. But on Wishbone Cay the light that illuminates the sea and sky for miles around is provided by a small, single flame reflected through a series of prisms. The source of energy is kerosene, and each night a lighthouse keeper walks up a hundred and one steps every two hours in order to replenish the kerosene and relight the flame. People here call it a living lighthouse and they love it just the way it is.

"Early this morning, around four o'clock the assistant lighthouse keeper, Winkley Wonkley, began walking up the circular stairway. But on this morning he heard a strange ticking coming from the basement. He walked down and spotted what looked like an alarm clock, as well as cans of paint, pulleys, boat line, a boatswain's chair, and a container of white powder. None of this had been there the previous day. Neither had the polka dots that now adorn the lighthouse. The lighthouse is locked except during daylight hours when people are invited to visit.

"Mr. Wonkley awoke the chief lighthouse keeper, Jaster Mookie, and both recalled hearing earlier what they believed to be quiet voices, but they didn't pay particular attention to them. Mr. Mookie called the chief of police, who in turn called the Coast Guard. Previous threats have been received concerning some American lighthouses, which the FBI and the CIA are currently investigating.

"Now let's go to Paula Zong in Washington."

"Good morning, Wolf. I'm with the President's press secretary, Airy Flusher. Mr. Flusher, what's the mood in Washington?"

"Very serious, Paula. The President is taking no chances, and has decided to mobilize the National Guard in order to seal off and protect every lighthouse in the United States. Can you imagine the chaos and damage that might result if our lighthouses were suddenly immobilized?

"The white powder is being sent to our laboratories in Miami for analysis. In the meantime, we are shipping to the Hopeful Harbour clinic by helicopter enough small pox vaccine to inoculate a thousand people, if necessary.

"Of course, the so-called alarm clock could be a timing device to set off a bomb to destroy the lighthouse and send a warning to the U. S. We are concerned that the apparent cans of paint could be bombs that would explode if opened. The bomb squad is checking them out now."

"Will the President announce a heightened state of alert?" asked Paula.

"I'm sure he will but we don't yet know what color it will be. There may be one color in areas around lighthouses, another color around port areas, and still another color for the remainder of the country."

Wolf Blitzed broke in. "Maybe he should declare a polka dot alert."

The press secretary replied dryly, "I don't think I'll pass that suggestion along to the President."

Paula continued. "That's not funny, Wolf. Mr. Flusher, what do you make of the polka dots?"

The press secretary shook his head. "We don't quite know what to make of it. It may have been some type of code to signal the beginning of certain acts of terrorism. Our cryptographers in the CIA are working on that now."

"Again, check the picture of the lighthouse. Notice that the colors of the Bahamian flag have been painted over the red and white stripes, which just happen to be symbols of the United States? This could be a message from a militant Bahamian splinter group being directed by El Qaeda, which seeks dominance over the United States. We've taken the lighthouse keeper into custody for questioning."

"Why have you done that," asked Wolf.

"Just as a precaution. 'Jaster' may be a Muslim name. One of our agents recalls a sheik by that name years ago. In addition, the lighthouse keeper named his eight-year old son, Muhammad."

"Maybe he was a big fan of Muhammad Ali," suggested Wolf.

"Maybe so, maybe not. What we do know is that he was very unhappy that the Bahamian Government wants to automate the Wishbone Cay Lighthouse, which would eliminate his job; and our government has been recommending automation of all lighthouses."

"Do you think this could have been just a prank by children?" asked Wolf.

"It's possible, but not likely. It's hard to get to the area, except by boat. The lighthouse is quite visible in the community and most likely children would be seen and recognized. All the lighthouse keeper's children were off at baseball camp, except his five-year own son and his five-year old nephew and someone that young could never have pulled off anything like this."

Harold started to jump up and object, but Benjy put his hand over his mouth and pulled him down.

"No," the Secretary went on, "This appears to be an act of deception well planned by experts."

Harold and Benjy gave one another high fives quietly and whispered, "Yes!"

Wolf interrupted, chuckling. "Could it be that the lighthouse itself is also involved in order to get more attention? After all, it is a living lighthouse?

"Wolf!" screamed Paula. "Have you been drinking pina coladas?"

"I don't drink pina coladas, Paula. They're too sweet," Wolf replied in a serious voice. The press secretary did not change expression.

"We have checked out this possibility, but haven't gotten any evidence that would implicate the lighthouse. What we have learned, though, is that the lighthouse keeper's young son and his cousin have been missing since this happened. We're concerned that they may be hostages."

"What are 'hostages?' whispered Benjy.

"I don't know. Maybe they're people who don't evacuate."

"We all pray for their safety. I know their parents must be frantic," said Wolf. "I'll be signing off now, but rest assured we'll be standing by until this is resolved."

"I'm sure you will, Blitz," replied Paula. "It's a tough assignment, but someone has to do it."

"Yes, Paula, but at least it beats Afghanistan. Wolf Blitzed, out."

Shortly after the TV crew departed, Condaleeza returned and began calling for the children. They emerged from under the house and were hugged wildly by Condaleeza.

"I'm so relieved to see you. Where were you?"

"We was hostages," replied Harold.

"My, my. Who was you hostages of?"

Benjy paused, "The terrorists."

Condleeza grabbed Benjy by the ear and began leading him into the house.

"You boys are about to see a little more terrorism. Benjy, what's this on the back of your ear? Why, it looks like yellow paint...and a little blue...and is that black? I never could get you to wash behind your ears."

Benjy decided to confess. He told her that they had painted the lighthouse. "But Leticia asked us to do it."

"Laytisha? A chicken asked you to paint the lighthouse?"

"Not a chicken, Mama. Leticia is really the lighthouse. She asked us to do it."

"Boy, are you telling me that the lighthouse talks? I'm getting you some of those pills tomorrow."

"She does, Mama. Ask her."

Condaleeza looked up at the lighthouse. "Laytisha! Did you ask these boys to paint your polka dots?" The lighthouse remained silent.

"Laytisha! I'll ask you just one more time, and if you don't answer now, these boys are getting a whuppin' they won't forget." The only noise heard was the sound of whimpering from Harold.

Condaleeza must have stood there for a full minute with her hand to her ear. Finally, she clapped her hands together, and laughed.

"It's o.k. Leticia, you can fess up." She gave the "thumbs-up" signal.

Leticia finally spoke. "Thank goodness, Condaleeza. I was afraid you would never give in."

"Mama! You have ESP," exclaimed Benjy.

"You watch your mouth, Boy! I bathed this morning...and I washed behind my ears!"

"No, Mama. I mean...you can hear Leticia talk."

"Honey, I have to confess. Leticia has been talking with me for years. I'm afraid we set you up. I knew she wanted a new outfit for Independence Day, but I didn't know how to get it for her. I was sure my special little boy would find a way, and you did."

Benjy smiled broadly, and then frowned. "But what are we going to do about getting Daddy home, and making all those other people go home?"

Condaleeza and Benjy took the next ferry over to Big Island and met with the police chief. He called the Coast Guard, which called the President's office, which said that there would be a meeting of the National Security Council later that day. Of, course, no one knows what is said at those meetings, but an unidentified source heard that a small faction led by the Attorney General wanted to extradite Harold and Benjy to the United States, try them for espionage as adults, and seek the death penalty.

Apparently cooler heads prevailed. Late that night a CIA agent disguised as a conch fisherman met with Condaleeza at a remote spot in the Bahama Flats called Porky Rock. Jaster was with him. About a half hour later, Condaleeza and Jaster got in their boat and returned to Hopeful Harbour, where they slept soundly.

"Good Morning, Americans. This is Wolf Blitzed, speaking once again from Hopeful Harbour where the Bahamians are celebrating Independence Day, just as we did about a week ago.

"We've moved our headquarters to a delightful bistro called Monsieur Jacques' where I'm enjoying a native breakfast of souse chicken, conch fritters, and a local beverage. The lighthouse sits directly across the harbor and she looks elegant, in an abstract sort of way. She now has a name, and it is Leticia.

"Since I spoke with you yesterday literally thousands of telegrams and email messages have poured in from all over the world, urging that the Prime Minister not automate the lighthouse. There have been demonstrations from Berkley, California to Paris, France, with participants chanting, "Let Leticia Live!" Paula, I understand you're with the President's press secretary, who has some late-breaking news."

"Yes, Wolf. What do you have for us, Mr. Flusher?"

"Thank you, Paula. Last night local police on the Big Island near Wishbone Cay engaged in a shootout with two Bahamian men they believe were attempting to blow up the dock facilities. Both men are dead, but the police are withholding identification. One of the bodies had several specks of paint remarkably similar to the paint found on the Wishbone Cay Lighthouse. The owner of the Wishbone Cay Club, which is near the lighthouse, confirmed that these men had stayed in a room there two nights earlier. Identities have not yet been confirmed. Since the men did not appear to be part of an international terrorist organization, the President has rescinded his order mobilizing the National Guard, but recommends that the American people maintain a high state of vigilance, particularly around coastal areas."

"Thank you. Mr. Flusher. That is a relief. Now back to you, Wolf."

"Thanks, Paula. I just want to report that the two missing boys are safe and had not been taken hostage. I'll be standing by at Monsieur Jacques' for my next assignment."

"I'm sure you will. This is Paula Zong. Good day."

Peace returned once more to Hopeful Harbour. The Prime Minister informed Hurricane Harry that any plans to automate the lighthouse have been suspended indefinitely. Leticia will keep her new outfit until the first of the year, when she will receive a new paint job. She's a happy lighthouse once again, as she knows that every two hours on every night, she will get lit.

HOPE TOWN LIGHTHOUSE HAIKU
Maureen Miller

Adorned in style and
Lit from pinnacle to ground
Christmas dressed lighthouse

December 2003

THIS DAY IS DONE
Maureen Miller

The red head
   glides gently into its western bed

Preparing for slumber
   pulling grey clouds behind
      like a small child with a blanket or sheet over head
   to ward off the cold – or monsters

Twilight lingers
   a nightlight
      to guide those boaters who have stretched the day
   back to safe harbor

The wind settles a bit
   leaving stillness in its path
birds fly to resting spots
   and mosquitoes disrupt
      the transparent peace

The lighthouse keeper climbs to the top
   and stokes the fires
      to announce the cold and heartless reefs below

There are few colors in the night sky blanket now
   some blue whites
   a streak of yellow
   and much grey

But the red head
   has gone to sleep once more

This day is done

January 2004

HOME

DOMICILE
Adelaide Cummings

I live in a house beside the sea.
And sea-sounds are a part of me.
Waves that slap against proud hull.
The loud, complaining wail of gull.
A flapping sail, a rigging's groan.
A halyard's twang, a motor's groan.
Wild geese honking through the sun
As the boats turn homeward, one by one...
The sounds of the sea roll over me.
This is my music, wild and free.
And there's nowhere else that I'd rather be.
For I live in a house beside the sea.

ULTRA-MARINE
Ann Corbitt

My new home rides upon a sea of greens,
Beyond which lies a larger sea of blues.
Gum elemi, sea grape, and buttonwood,
Acacia, guava, tamarind
Wear different hues: viridian, deep malachite,
Kelly, soft sage, silver gray.
The farther ocean's azure, cobalt,
Violet, cerulean, in ever-shifting shades.

When winds or breezes
Riffle leaves and waves,
I cannot always tell
Which is the surf
And which my neighbor's palms.

February 2003

RAINBOWS OUT MY WINDOW
Mary Balzac

Rainbows viewed the past two mornings
Outside my western window,
While reading the news on my Toshiba laptop
Remind me once more how blessed
I am in living on this tiny island
On the edge of a continental shelf.

Last night lounging on upstairs deck
Glass of Pinot Gris in hand, I watched
The full moon slowly vanish beneath
The shadow of this planet gravity holds me to.
Light clouds added to the magical event.
Ocean waves sang in the near distance.

Lizard, twisting his head looks up as I walk in,
"Does she really let me live here in this house?
I think of "One Toe" the little splay foot who
Lives at Lory's on the window ledge.
"Yes, Splay Foot, you are welcome in my home
You do eat mosquitoes and ants, don't you?"

And, Old Ribbit, sitting on the awning
Windowpane, outside, over the kitchen sink
"Do you enjoy your feast during the annual
Invasion of little black bugs?"

Rainbows, stars, lunar eclipse
Ocean sounds, mosquitoes' buzz.
Yard needs weeding; windows need washing
Floor needs sweeping; all can wait
As I meditate on lizards, frogs,
Rainbows and lunar eclipses.

November 2003

Return to Hope Town
Slender striped tower welcomes
Celebrating home!

Return to Hope Town
Friendly faces wreathed in smiles
Blessings bounce around

Return to Hope Town
Phone dead – Lister down – 'fridge dark
Love this island life?

Nan Kenyon
December 2003

ABACO HAIKU
Ann Corbitt

Hiss and smash of surf
Against the coral cliffs outside
Soothes me into sleep.

January 2002

PEOPLE AND PERSONALITIES

THE CHARACTER OF HOPE TOWN: THEODORE
Larry Beachy

Old timers say that at one time, over eleven hundred people lived between where Vernon's Grocery is now located and the Lodge. Houses were very close together and the kitchens were a separate little building from the living quarters. Outdoor ovens were located in every yard and all kinds of breads and pies could be seen baking in them. Fires were devastating because of the winds and the closeness of the dwellings. Volunteer firemen fought them using hand pumps and bucket brigades.

We still have a very fine volunteer fire department but it is much better equipped with modern re-breathing devices and protective clothing. Heavy-duty pumps supply fresh or salt water to the fire locations now. Progressive property owners living near the water are even installing dry hydrants with extensions out into the sea. These hydrants provide a convenient way for the pumps to hook up and provide water.

Depending upon whether you were from the southern United States or were of British persuasion, the Law was provided by a 'sheriff' or a 'constable.'

It's been said that you really are not accepted in Hope Town unless Donny Cash gives you nickname. Donny works at Elbow Cay Rentals and is a handsome, local boy that was born and raised in Hope Town. He can recite the genealogical as well as social history of every local and their family. Donny has that unique ability to remember all the little slips, bumps and skids that everyone goes through trying to grow up in a tightly knit community. Donny doesn't tolerate airs by the genteel. Instead he greets everyone with a good-natured smile and an all-knowing look of understanding.

My wife Carol and I decided to stop in at Captain Jack's for a little libation and quick bite. We had just passed through the door and were going down the bar exchanging pleasantries and high fives when I heard a loud and clear Bahamian voice call out

"Everybody get out your ID. Here comes the Sheriff and he's got Iris with him." Immediately we were no longer Carol and Larry Beachy; we were not even Mr. Larry and Miss Carol. No, we had been dubbed, The Sheriff and Iris by the Master of Nicknames Donny Cash.

Theodore Malone had been the sheriff of Hope Town for many, many, years. His wife Iris and his mother operated an ice cream shop, the only one in town. Theodore also was one of the first to rent bicycles in Hope Town. So Theodore was not only the provider of law and order but he was an enterpriser and here is where the stories began.

Carol and I purchased Theodore and Iris's home about ten years ago. I had known Theodore for many years and was accustomed to seeing him in his uniform walking the streets of Hope Town. His house had a splendid location as far as Carol and I were concerned. Neighbors claimed that if the termites stopped holding hands the house would fall down. We started our labor of love but found it was almost impossible to work a full day with out being interrupted by well meaning Hope Townians who just had to share a Theodore story. It reminded me of Fibber McGee and Molly on the old Majestic radio when I was a kid.

Victor Patterson stopped by and searched the wall across from the side door to the south. There had to be a hole in the wall where an arrow was shot through the window in the door, traveled across the room and stuck in the wall. Seems that the Sheriff was making it uncomfortable for a couple of characters in Hope Town. Someone had taped a message to an arrow and shot it through the south window in the door. As nearly as I could find out, the message pretty much warned Theodore to mind his own business. I could never find the hole or the results of the message, but I am sure it was impressive.

That door was a very important door because it was through it that homemade chocolate and vanilla ice cream was sold. The story goes that you had to be careful of the ice incorporated in the ice cream. Many times you got more back in change than you what paid for the cone. Young men would wait until Theodore's mother was running the cash register, which was a cupcake tray with various coins in it. Her education in math was not the strongest and if the kids were patient there was a good chance they would come out ahead.

Theodore had a number of children and his full share of boys. Many of them are quite successful as adults, however not everyone thinks it was necessarily due to Theodore's influence. Like the time he confiscated a full bale of marijuana and locked it up in the jail downtown below the post office near the commissioners office. Somehow the jail was unlocked and the bale of marijuana disappeared. Theodore guarded the keys carefully and always kept them in his house. No one had access to the keys but Theodore, Iris and well, maybe the boys.

It seems Theodore kept a heavy hand on some people. Some say they got blamed for things that they should not have been blamed for. Others say they had it coming. One of these young man felt he had enough of Theodore's hounding. He walked past Theodore's front door and saw him sitting in his recliner beside his mother. The angry young man stopped at his uncle's and borrowed a 410 shotgun, loaded it and fired it through the front door. Theodore yelled,

"Mommy, Mommy, get down!"

The young man thought he had killed Theodore's mother. He went up another half a block, stopped and shot himself, a terrible, terrible suicide in Hope Town.

An old corrugated building was in the backyard. Odell Bethel, my neighbor, asked if he could tear the building down and make lobster condos out of the salvaged tin. I thought that was a great idea and perhaps Odell would take me along to look for those spineys. When I returned I found an old, red narrowed-tier bicycle sitting in my back yard. Odell had found it inside. It wasn't long until "Tattoo" Russell was walking beside my place and he called out,

"That is my bicycle. Theodore took it away from me when I was 13 years old and never gave it back."

I replied that I had been looking for the owner and if he would step through my gate he could collect his now rusty bicycle with two flat tires. I'd made another friend.

When you hear at one of the local bars, "Here comes the Sheriff and Iris," just remember, titles don't come easy.

April 2004

TO ADELAIDE
Janet Pearce Foster

Just a note
With thanks for your vote
In our favor

And with our hope
That later
You savor
Some time
Sublime
With me and he
On the sea
Of Abaco
Where we'll go
I do not know

So *merci beaucoup*
For all that you do
To inspire and guide
Those of us who try
For as full a life
In one day
As Adelaide

DEDICATED TO THE HOPE TOWN WRITERS' CIRCLE
Irv Gubitz

Many of us are enriched by moonlight walks on the beach
And the sun's sparkling through forests and green fields
We use words and verse to chronicle our joys and deepest sorrows.
We invite the world to join with our laughter, awe and tears

But many others never share with us, and seem to have no voice.
Yet surely life provokes in everyone the need to speak, smile and cry.
Where do they live and work, those quiet ones who don't speak to us?
It seems odd that it falls just to us to give voice to the speechless ones.

It isn't arrogance by those of us who speak in odes and paragraphs,
And who seem to say our thoughts are more intense that all the rest.
Even if they toil in mines and tunnels or shops and stalls
They breathe as we do, and know as we do, that life has many colors.

So let our tales and sonnets peak to all the world.
Then little ones laugh, middle ones smile and older ones grin and nod.
Our words must resound in widespread places and to all those other People.
And the we can know that with our pad and pens we speak not to,
But for them all.

THE CHARACTER OF HOPE TOWN: MISS LILLY
Larry Beachy

Moving to Hope Town from Lubbers Quarters was much more of a cultural shock than my wife Carol and I could ever have suspected. Hope Town, "A quaint little drinking town with a fishing problem," read the bumper sticker. The town certainly had lots of character but it was also full of individual characters.

Living on Lubbers Quarters since 1980, we came to Hope Town for most of our services. Willard and Susanne Bethel, and Vernon Malone provided our groceries for us. Theodore Malone was the Constable. Sherlock Russell would greet us along the street. However we were soon to learn about one of Hope Town's characters without warning.

Sunday morning 5:00 a.m. and Carol and I were sleeping upstairs in our little Bahamian cottage. The downstairs is in the process of being gutted. Floors, walls, ceilings, everything was "being pulled down and carried," as the Bahamians describe it.

"Wake up, wake up. Listen, I hear a police car siren," I told Carol one morning.

Sure enough, coming in our upstairs window we could hear a European type of emergency siren moving through the streets of Hope Town. Up and down, loud and soft, but no question about it, there was an emergency vehicle on the loose in Hope Town. I opened the window wide looking for smoke, surely there was a fire, it must be the fire engine.

No smoke could be seen or smelled. The siren stopped, but only for a moment. It started in full volume right at the beginning of our sidewalk that runs by the side of our house. Actually this sidewalk is called Albury's Street in Hope Town and these little streets add to the character of Hope Town.

Right underneath my window at 5:00 a.m. a person passed emitting the most god-forsaken combination of a wail and a scream. It alternated between loud and high pitch to soft and low pitch depending on the breathing that was taking place at the time of the emitting. Just as she passed under my window I made out some words,

"Here Snowflake. Here snowflake." on and on she went, her voice trailing all over the settlement.

To describe her you will need to recall Lil' Abner's mother in Dog Patch as she was depicted by Al Capp, one of the greatest satirists of our time. Standing straight as a board with the most bizarre clothing combination you can imagine, was a small, skinny lady wearing thick glasses and a pair of hose that had seen better days last year.

My neighbor, the builder/owner of Hope Town's only apartment house (which also adds character to the settlement) yelled out his window.

"Lilly, that damn Snowflake died three years ago. Go back home and shut up."

Ah ha! I had met my first Hope Town Character, Miss Lilly the Cat Lady. I discovered that she was my neighbor living next door to Harbour View Grocery in an old, run-down, decrepit house owned by her mother. She also provided a home for twenty cats. Thus, she rightly earned her title The Cat Lady and, of course, her house was referred to as the Cat Lady's House. Many times the 'Lady' was dropped.

Miss Lilly passed on a few years back from a combination of asthma and other complications. The nurse would get a couple of fireman and they would corner Miss Lilly in the grocery store or her house and give her a shot for her asthma. No one, of course, could force her to take her medication for schizophrenia so most of the time Miss Lilly wandered the community a completely uncontrolled paranoid schizophrenic. One day she might be observed walking in her characteristic manner, stiff-armed, decked out in a cast-off garments, holding a large butcher knife, swearing at the top of her lungs. If you had enough courage to inquire what was wrong, she would tell you about those so-and-so kids that locked her in her out house, which still stands today. I am sure it never dawned on any parents to teach their children to be kind to Miss Lilly any more then it dawned on the parents to treat Miss Lilly as a mentally deficient adult.

Once the Constable showed up at my house and said he needed to conduct an inspection for marijuana growing in my garden. Now sometimes I wish my retirement provided for me a little better but never have I undertaken the growing of illegal drugs to supplement my income. Upon inquiry, I discovered that Miss Lilly had turned me in to the police. Here is a lady that wandered the streets screaming for a dead cat or swearing at children carrying a butcher knife and yet she was cognizant of the procedure for turning in her neighbor.

Various locals told me that Miss Lilly had been sent to Nassau to be evaluated and perhaps put in a home for mentally handicapped. She always returned with a clean report: patient suitable for living in society. Lilly was much smarter than she let on. We finally realized that when Carol and I hauled away two truckloads of junk from our neighbor's property, Miss Lilly was afraid we were going to start on her place. So she turned us in.

Lilly lived in squalor to say the least. Her floors were matted with old newspapers, food cartons, empty water jugs and cat dung. Once or twice a year a couple of local gals would lure her off to Man-O-War and go in and clean and haul truckloads of junk away. Lilly would return, throw her fit and proceed to rebuild a house-sized litter box. Well-meaning foreigners would donate money to some animal lovers who would trap Miss Lilly's cats and take them over and have them spayed. Still, she managed to have one or two that were pregnant most of the time. These adorable kittens would attract tourists who would give Lilly free cigarettes and money for cokes.

The locals tell me Miss Lilly was normal and very smart, until she got into her late teens. Some say she started reading books about witchcraft and became very mean and abusive to her mother. In fact, during the late teens is when schizophrenia usually shows up so I doubt that there was any dark side or witchcraft in Lilly's tormented life.

I tried to help Lilly whenever I could. She once had a toothache and asked me to look at it. I have done many autopsies and forensic work for the coroners in Saint Joe and Elkhart Counties but never have I looked into a mouth that looked like Miss Lily's. I am not sure if the tears in my eyes were from sympathy or from the terrible odor that hit me like a sledgehammer during that examination.

After Miss Lilly died, a sympathetic group held a memorial. I went, not to memorialize Miss Lilly, after all who could ever forget her, but to see who would come. I was amazed at the people that showed up and clustered around that foul, infested building she called home. Her cats, now numbering well above twenty, peered out from cracks, under floors, and next-door buildings. Each one was as wild and scared as the day it was born. I have never known Lilly to own what you and I would call a pet cat. Wonderful eulogies were given. Many good things were said about Lilly. I couldn't stop thinking where were these people in her life? Were these the people that allowed her to live under these conditions? Maybe it was their conscience that made them say the words coming out of their mouths.

April 2004

THE SEA

ABACO HAIKU
Ann Corbitt

Conquering the reefs
Sea panzers, steaming spray, roll
Relentless toward shore

December 2001

NEAR THE SOUND OF WATER
Audrey Malone

When we chose a subject to write about to exchange with our writer friends in England, we never thought that "Our Favourite Place" would be so hard to write about. I think each one of us is having a hard time getting it down to one specific place.

Sometimes I think my favourite place is inside my head, in my imagination, but I have chosen mine as 'near the sound of water' and that can be a lot of places.

I like to sit on the bench on the sand dunes and watch and listen to the waves as they gently run along the beach; my book is forgotten as I let the sound lull me into peaceful imaginations.

In my bed at night in a storm, I hear the ocean's angry roar. For some years I didn't know what the ocean roar was and learned it's not the gentle swishy-swash on a calm day but awash continually echoing across the dunes, then across the island and into my window.

But probably my very favourite sound of water is the gentle lapping on a sailboat's sides as she sails quietly through the blue-green water to nowhere.

March 2004

A simple walk upon the beach
How were we to know
We'd make a find beyond our reach,
Which wouldn't let us go.

New to lovely Elbow Cay,
Living on a boat.
Feet splashing in the turquoise sea,
Strange thing right there afloat.

Big and black, a bulky find,
The truth began to dawn.
We poked and ripped and looked behind,
What trouble this could spawn!

Tug, sniff, nervous looks some more,
Are people there unseen?
We walk away, it sits on shore
Say or not, we're in between.

Tell the law, the man Malone
What will he think of us?
Strangers here, so far from home,
Should we create a fuss?

The Post Office, no privacy there,
Oh dear, should we go hide?
Miss Flossie's ears grow quite large I swear,
As we beckon Theodore outside.

Describe and point we spill our tale,
Relief it's done, it's through.
The Constable puts it in jail,
Someone says "I heard 'bout you."

So, found a square grouper did you?
Doesn't happen just every day.
Grape vine's not slow, people have a clue,
Be sure to watch where you play.

The story's not over, so sad to tell,
More happened that very dark night.
Young fellows with bolt cutters got into jail,
Liberated and sold it out of sight.

Twenty years later and we've learned a heap,
Now we're quite sure when we say.
Next time cut it open, pull it out in the deep,
Let salt water do damage right away

Kitty Clark

BOTTLE MAIL
Audrey Malone

A letter in a bottle went skipping over the waves
Two lonely sailors wrote that message
Hoping someone would walk a beach
And find it washed up there
It drifted on the ocean
No cay or island it could find
It saw a pod of whales playing in the waves
Some seagulls checked to see
If maybe a fish was underneath
A lonely frigate bird soared overhead
It didn't look like food so it flew past
A dolphin family played sink-the-bottle
The brave bottle stayed afloat
It drifted, weeks, months,
Once some land it saw, a breeze blew it away
It drifted, lonely, waiting, waiting,
One calm night with no waves to rock it to sleep
It saw a light, in the distance, flashing
Oh my! It thought land may be near
If only I could reach a beach
Someone will find my message there
It finally fell asleep, awaking at sunrise
Safely lying on a white sand beach.
Someone comes along the beach
Looks like a blue-eyed sailor man
Who likes to walk the beach, be near the sea
He stooped, picked up the bottle and saw the letter there
Carefully he took the letter out and read the message
Oh! Said he a letter from a young man
I'll take it to my daughter
And she can make a new friend
So the lonely little bottle
Smiled happily in the bright Bahamian sun
It had got its letter safely across a great wide ocean
To a tiny island and a lonely blonde haired lady
Forty years have come and gone since
And that lonely sailor and blond haired lady
Have yet to meet

2002

FLOTSAM
Beti Webb

The sea spews up detritus
On the sand
Regurgitates from her depths
What people throw away.
With her prodigious alchemy
She transmutes dross
Polishes a broken branch
Into a driftwood sculpture
Turns a broken bottle
Into sea glass gem.
Flotsam and jetsam
Come with every tide,
Oddments transmogrified,
Gifts transformed by time
As offerings to the world.

Alert to possibilities,
Serendipity's potentialities,
I walk the beach
In search of treasures
Flung up by the waves
Gifts from the deep
To meld into my life.

March 2002

SEA GLASS AND SEASHELLS
Mary Balzac

BEC, BatelCo and Out Island Inter.Net
Cable Bahamas and Coral Wave
Inside Outside and Pinder's Plumbing
While living in Paradise to these I've become slave.

Phone calls and more phone calls get me nowhere,
I yell, scream, or plead with a deferential please
Still nothing happens, not in my control
It's all so upsetting, I feel no ease.

What can I do? Well, I can walk the beach.
Gather sea glass and seashells and find my own peace.

All over the planet are war cries and war clouds.
To march against war will not be allowed.
A federal judge states that only a rally can gather
In Dag Hammarskjold Square. So in order to matter,
I hope they'll dare to raise placards for peace
And march through New York, so the war cries can cease.

Disconnects, no service, faucets still dripping
Make me wonder, am I flipping
Out of my mind, as frustration takes over?
Nothing gets done...I have no control.
But what can I do? I'm not very bold...

To the beach I can go once more to walk
With a friend and share sunrise as we amble and talk
Watch seabirds in seaweed. Save a beached crab from disaster.
Catch up with our happenings. Lighten up with laughter.

Look at the beauty in sea glass and seashells
And know deep down inside, somehow, all is well.

February 2003

SELF ESTEEM
Irv Gubitz

I walked the beach last night
Casting sharp precise shadows
From the clear and brilliant moon.
My footprints in the sand traced the journey
And left evidence of my being.

The morning sun obscured my moon shadow.
Through the hours the tide erased my footprints.
No question of my ever being there; no doubt of what I've done.
I've been there and I know it, and carry its luster in my heart.
You can't deny me, Sun. You can't erase me, Tide.

MY SECRET
Beti Webb

Last year it was - a day of raging winds
That shrieked and whistled like a soul in pain,
And blew through all the timbers of the house
Not stuffed with sacking, (to keep out the rain)

No fishermen would venture out that day;
But when they heard the cry of 'wreck ashore,'
They rushed to man the boats through mighty waves,
My husband, Job, as always to the fore.

The salvage was a livelihood to us,
But when he heard a ship had come to grief
'Twould be, to Job, his very first concern
To pluck the drowning sailors from the reef.

"The ship broke up and all were drowned," Job said.
"I even saw a woman swept ashore."
He brought his share of salvage in a sack
And spread it out before me on the floor.

And there, amid the drabness of my home,
I saw this thing of beauty - good as new -
A graceful vase full-fashioned out of glass,
In gleaming shades of red and gold and blue.

Job saw I loved the vase, but shook his head,
He wrapped it, and returned it to the sack.
"Though the Customs take all this," he said
"We'll get our share of salvage money back."

The inspector looked around our shabby house
"Now, are you sure I've got the lot?" he said.
He little knew I'd hid the precious vase
Beneath the mattress of my baby's bed.

Unknown to Job, it's when I'm on my own
And everything feels drab and worn and old,
I take it out and put it in the sun
To glimmer like a jewel laced with gold.

And if that tragic girl who lost her life
Could know I'd saved her treasure from the sea
By hiding it below my sleeping child,
I'm sure that she'd look down and smile at me.

March 2002

THE SEA
Audrey Malone

The sea, the sea
I must go out on the sea again
Where the deep green water can envelop my soul
And wrap around my starving body like a blanket,
Where I can store into its dark green depth,
And let it feed me its ambrosia, soft, soothing.
Where did I get this need of water?
The salty smell, the rocking waves,
Sounds of the surf, lulling me to sleep.
Was it from my ancestor?
Who was shipwrecked on my island home?
Where he fell in love and stayed.
My grandfather whose love for the sea
Led him to build boats to sail far and wide.
In later years, my uncle,
Who built spectacular and famous boats
Without the help of any master plan.
His love of ships guiding his hands and heart
To form and shape, and carve these masterpieces
He made strong boats to carry freight
To the United States, to Cuba, To Nassau,
Sailed by our island sailor men, my father too
He made small sailing boats
To sail for pleasure, by those others who love the sea
Where did I get this need of water?
The need to be on the green ocean waves
I think it was from my ancestors
When they stepped aboard those ships
And left their British homeland
To find a new home on these Isles of June.
I'm glad they came.

December 2002

BOATS

A DREAM
Audrey Malone

A dream come true
To sail a tall ship on the sea
A beautiful ship,
Paint sparkling in the sun,
Her lines so beautifully shaped
With loving hands,
I hear the waves caress the bow,
Peaceful voices, contented sailors,
In love with sea, sun, and sails,
Uncle Will, I feel your gentle spirit
Blowing in the sails
As clear green water
Slips beneath her keel,
The world's at peace
Just for a day
My dreams came true, Uncle Will
I sailed your lovely schooner
Named for you. *William H. Albury*

March 2002

POINTING
Irv Gubitz

It's so nice to come across the hill and stroll down to the harbor,
Especially when all the boats point right to me as if in greeting.
But there are times when they point to the left or to the right
As if attracted more by someone else.

Worst of all is when they turn completely away,
No longer interested in me.
What makes them change their directions and attitudes?
Is it something I said or did that caused such reaction?

Must I take the blame when unseen forces impose themselves
Upon the crowd? Who hears tides? Who sees a wind?
Who knows what shapes everyone's directions?

Yet sometimes there is one out there which ignores the rest of the fleet
And stays looking toward me, like a friend.
I always like that one, whether it's a ketch, a sloop or a skiff.
Then I tip my hat and smile toward the harbor, feeling welcome.

THE SCHOONER *ONE DAY*
Janet Pearce Foster

In the bow of a handmade boat
Wooden, solid and sound
I feel safe, secure
Serene as she ploughs
Through God's heaven on earth,
That fluid world
Of iridescent creatures
And littered wrecks
Called into eternity

The stem rises and falls
Making waves into clouds
Their breath stirs the wisps of my hair
While I rest
In the womb
Of my own vessel

ABACO DINGHY
Audrey Malone

There she sits
A thing of beauty
Lovingly shaped and crafted
With gifted hands and eyes
Her graceful lines are smooth
Her varnish sparkling
Her mast stands tall
Her boom swings free
Her rudder still, waiting
For white sails to sail the seas
There she sits
A thing of beauty
An Abaco Dinghy.

March 2002

SEASONS

BACK YARD SPRING
Mary Balzac

Bird feeder's almost empty
Many visitors today
Certainly a sign
Spring is on its way.

Banana quits hog the feeder
A hummingbird hovers near
With furiously whirring wings
Banana quits disappear.

Hummingbird descends in flight
Landing, assuages her thirst.
Now joined by another
A brighter throat than the first.

Beyond the feeder I see
New blossoms on the key lime tree
New tender green shoots
On the ruby red grapefruit.

March winds now blow
I fertilize for fruit and flowers
Birds, you better start building your nests
Will we have April showers?

March 2003

HOPE TOWN IN JUNE
Steve Best

I like Hope Town in June, how about you?
I like a Buffet tune, how about you?
I like the harbor side when a storm is due,
Moonlight on quiet seas, shimmered by an ocean breeze,
How about you?
I savor Vernon's bread, can't get my fill,
And even Willard's looks give me a thrill.
Meeting friends at the public dock,
Church chimes at six o'clock,
May not be new,
Still, I like it, how about you?

Hope Town in March, as well, busy and gay,
Art shows, conch fritters smell, Heritage Day.
Meeting old chums again on the Queen's highway,
Never too rushed to chat, talking of this and that,
Day after day
I watch the old lighthouse breaking the night,
Always a comforting, glorious sight
Beams stroke the harbor side
Giving the village pride,
Each day anew,
And I like it, how about you?

Sometimes the power's gone, we're left in the dark,
Generators turning on, dogs start to bark
When hearing sounds again of a gathering storm,
Sages Draconian of rages Abaconian
Hardly the norm
Vernon's all out of bread, planes cease their flight,
Winds howl and folks scowl into the night,
As frogs croak and mice poke, roosters crow, too,
They like it, how about you?

The sound of silence emanates from every phone,
VHF is going dead, can't get a moan,
Everything begins to rust, or else it smells of must.
Complaining won't cure it, so I just endure it;
How about you?
There go the lights again, telephones ring,
And the smell of Vernon's bread, banana quits sing,
We're back in harmony, looks like it's going to be
A Hope Town day,
Still, I like it, any old way.

HUMMINGBIRD LOVE
Mary Balzac

Wee hummingbird visits the red-based feeder
Outside the screened porch, feeder filled
With one-fourth dilute boiled sugar water
Meant to entice for my pleasurable viewing
Iridescent hummingbirds and yellow-bellied banana quits.

Stopping for a moment on my way out the screened door,
I send love, heart to heart, toward this wee being
I've been told this is how to communicate
With those of differing species than my own
A practice session for loving (I'm tired of reading of war).

A good place to start is with this wee small bird,
Perched on the feeder edge dipping his beak
In and out as he drinks. I stand...
Concentrating on heart to heart...
The hummingbird stops sipping, stands still...

Stops sipping, stands still...so still...
Turning toward me as we continue
In silent heart communication
And time, as we know it stops...until...
Across the open garden from thick bush

A furious whirring of wings, a stop in mid air, almost
Colliding with my wee friend.   A quick hummingbird
Scolding ensues.   With barely a backward glance
(I would have missed it if I blinked) off they fly
An iridescent pair in jet speed flight.

Hey, there, I have no intent to steal your mate
You jealous tiny iridescent being.   I was just
Sharing a moment's heart to heart.   Please,
Do join us next time. So much nicer than
Jealous acts or reading of possible war.

February 2003

Abaco Haiku
Ann Corbitt

Palm fronds whispering
In warm breezes confide
Their tropical secrets.

Palmettoes natter,
Palm fronds whisper, as the wind
Prompts conversation.

Indigo sky pierced
By myriad points of light...
Such immensity!

January 2002

INDEPENDENCE DAY
Steve Best

A score and a decade ago the Bahamas
Became independent for papas and mamas,
Whose long ago papas and mamas were seized
From their homes and sold. Dramas
Of cruelty and heartache as these
Poor people, now slaves, were carried 'cross seas
As chattels, like cattle, to build a new land;
Not for themselves, but like sand
For a beach, grains trampled down,
Supporting a master supporting the Crown.

First they brought the papas and mamas
To the American colonies, not the Bahamas,
To work the land, pick the cotton,
Longing for freedom, but misbegotten.
An ironic stroke brought them here,
Many masters held freedom dear,
And fought to shed the British yoke,
And thus become independent folk.
But the loyal ones took their papas and mamas,
And headed for the Island Bahamas.

They worked the land, planted cotton,
But as we know the plants turned rotten,
As did slavery, and soon each nation
Decided to grant emancipation.
Master and slave became the same,
But without elections, just in name,
They felt; and still they longed to be
Independent, like you and me.
And without a fight they were fully free
On the tenth of July of seventy-three.

Personally speaking, I love two nations,
And cherish our continuing good relations,
We Yanks say we're so patriotic,
But half of us vote,; that's idiotic.
We should take a lesson from this island nation
With almost total participation.
If you talk the talk, you should walk the walk,
And defend with fervor the right to squawk.
For dual independence I proudly speak,
My celebration lasts a week.

July 2003

TALES OF HURRICANES

FRANCES
Karen F. Huff-Lowe

My namesake is fast approaching, packing winds of 125 mph, expecting to increase in strength. Once again, just like with Floyd, I have the gut-wrenching feeling this hurricane is coming right for us. I can't sleep. What do I do? Stay or evacuate? Of course, my family in the States is pressuring me to get off the island and come home. Knowing how stubborn I am, they remind me hurricanes kill and it is my responsibility to get my children to safety. They also remind me that I was lucky to get out of here with Floyd and don't delay making airline reservations. They don't want me waiting until the last minute and being one of the last planes out again.

I don't know, but no time to think about it now, dawn has broken and there are shutters to put on the houses, whirly-birds to be removed from the roofs, articles in the yard need to be stowed away, boats to secure, laundry to finish, flashlights to check for operation, on and on, the amount of work to get done in a short period of time is mind-boggling. All the while, we must continuously monitor The Weather Channel for the latest on the intensity and track of Hurricane Frances.

The decision looms in the back of my mind as the chores slowly get done and our properties, like the rest of Hope Town looks like a ghost town boarded up tight. A coffee break and again, I am back to the decision process. I turn to my husband for guidance. With Floyd, there was no question, take the kids and get the hell out of here. This time, it is "go if you'd like, but I don't think you need to. The kids are older now and this one isn't as bad as Floyd."

I am shocked by his response. I guess I fully expected him to tell me to leave again. Now, I am really puzzled. Is he not concerned for our safety? Does he not want to be alone and face the aftermath alone? Why is he not pushing me to go again? The tug of war inside me increases and guilt sets in. I don't want to leave my husband and have him face this beast alone. I remember, all too well, the shell-shocked gaze in the faces of everyone who experienced Floyd and its aftermath, the zombie effect of spinning wheels because there is so much to do you don't know where to start. The discomforts of no power, no telephones, repetitious canned meals, the overwhelming sadness of loss and the agony of not being able to communicate with loved ones in the States. I don't want my husband to carry this burden alone. But I also remember, the emotional trauma and scars my children bear from Floyd. I don't want to inflict any more pain on them. Is it better to stay so there isn't any separation and they won't worry about their father or should I take them out of harm's way? What do I do? Regardless of my decision, it would be wise to make arrangements to leave, so I do, just in case.

I'm not feeling well; must be the stress and the fact that I haven't slept for two nights. The third night is approaching and I still don't know what to do, but the time has come; I have to make a decision. Tomorrow is the final day and my last chance to evacuate. Frances is now a Category 4 storm, with winds of 135 mph. I turn to my children advising them the final decision rests with their father and me, but I would like their input and to know how they feel about the upcoming storm.

My eldest son, Stony, advises that he wants to stay and experience it, but on the other hand he sorta' wants to go, well he's not sure – I understand his anxiety completely. He's torn, just as I am. I reassure him it is okay to have mixed emotions about the situation but he needs to understand that if I go, he and his brother will go with me.

My youngest, Eli, who bears the deepest scars of Floyd, wants to go; he's scared. I know he doesn't really understand exactly what he's afraid of but his memories are still fresh and very real.

He asks me, "Mom, if we go, can I take my bear out of his special keepsake box and take him with us?"

"Of course," I say.

"As a matter of fact, you can take him out this evening and sleep with him if that would make you feel better."

I am comforted by the big smile that crosses my child's face. My husband reiterates that I have his blessings to go, but he doesn't think I need to. Aaahhh – no help.

I am still wrestling with the decision. I don't want to leave my husband but I don't want my children traumatized again. I give up – I can't decide – I put it, the decision, in God's hands. I tuck the children in bed, tell God my struggle and ask Him to help me – give me a sign if you will – I plea and lay my head down to rest. Surely sleep will come easy, it has to come. I am emotionally and physically exhausted.

At 3 a.m. my youngest child wakes me informing me he had a bad dream about the hurricane. Eli climbs in bed with us and settles back to sleep. I drift off again as well, thanking God for my sign. First thing in the morning, I'll pack our bags.

The next morning we head across the Sea of Abaco and it is rough. Eli, with Bear safely tucked under his arm, asks if this is the hurricane. Upon arriving at the airport an hour and fifteen minutes ahead of the scheduled 11 a.m. flight departure, they tell me they were waiting on us to clear so we could fly out sooner. They are ready to close the airport and need my plane to take off in order to do so. The necessary papers are exchanged and we load the plane.

Jeep Byers is sitting in the seat in front of me. I remark that he must have come over on the 8 a.m. ferry to beat me here. He told me there was no ferry service today; he slept over on Marsh Harbour. No wonder we were the only souls out on the treacherous Sea of Abaco this morning.

Jeep and I begin to reminisce about Hurricane Floyd and are glad to be getting off the island. Just as we are ascending, the pilot comes on the speaker.

"Here's the deal with our fuel situation."

What? Did I hear him correctly? Is he playing Russian roulette with my and my children's lives not to mention with everyone else on this plane? Is he nuts? What drugs is he on? There are no deals with fuel when you are 10,000 feet off the ground – what does he think he is doing? I want off this plane.

The pilot continues.

"We had planned to refuel here however, they have already secured the fuel truck on higher ground and it is blocked in by other cars and the owners can't be reached, so we couldn't get fuel in Marsh Harbour.

"Technically, I have just enough fuel to get us back to Daytona, but I wouldn't have the additional 45 minutes of extra flying time capacity that is required by law, therefore, we have called Freeport and they are holding off closing the airport until we get there and refuel. They had already parked their fuel truck but have retrieved it and are waiting for our arrival to refuel. Sorry for the delay and extra stop but it shouldn't take too long."

I guess not, but Jeep and I both agree, if we don't get fuel in Freeport, we're off this plane. I will resort to Plan B, just conceived. We will get off and go wait out this storm with my sister-in-law who is in Freeport waiting to have a baby. However, I prefer to go home to South Carolina because I think the storm is gonna' curve, hitting Abaco with the worst right front quadrant and then pass directly over Grand Bahama.

Fortunately, we fueled up and headed down the runway again. Talk about getting out by the skin of your teeth – we watched them close the door again: two airports shutting down as we depart.

As we descend over Daytona, I see that I-95 is bumper-to-bumper and if they are moving it is at a snail's pace. A1A looks okay, but I think it will be more crowded as people try to get away from the coastline. I will go with my original plan of taking the old inland country roads, the ones I traveled to Florida on when I was a kid. The last thing I want is to get stuck in a bottleneck on the roads when I have at least nine hours of driving ahead of me. I know the hotels are already all booked up so if I get stuck and can't make it all the way, I'll have to stop and call on help from friends along the way. If they aren't home, I guess it means having a few 'zzz's in a rest area parking lot, which I would rather not do. At 2:15 p.m., I call my sister and leave a message.

"We are leaving Dayton airport now. Will call again when we stop for dinner to advise our status."

Little did I know, our journey has just begun...

HURRICANE FRANCES PASSES THROUGH
Audrey Malone

Reports are Hurricane Francis is, after all; she is making a direct path through the Bahamas. I think about what to do; I feel so alone in these kinds of times since Benjie died, although I know I do have family and friends who watch out for me.

Finally Frances is in the Bahamas and not predicted to turn anytime soon. We prepare as best we can as the wind starts to pick up. Wayne says after work he will help me put up my shutters. I can put most of them up by myself but need help for a couple of the higher ones. I don't intend to put any on the windows next to Vernon's house because that side is sheltered. When I get home, Vernon had sent Jack and he has my house all cinched up (as we say when everything is closed up tight) even Kat Ballou's escape window. I immediately take it down as that one is on the sheltered side and I can communicate with Vernon next door.

The wind is picking up and I try to move things away from the windows as best I can and then cook supper as I know BEC will turn the power off when the winds reach forty miles an hour. The winds continue to pickup and the power goes off; I go to bed. I slept a little and get up at daylight to howling winds and rain, shingles had blown off and water was pouring in. I gathered every kind of container I had in my house and put them under the drips. They helped some but water was splattering everywhere. At my back bedroom door, the water was pouring in under the top facings. I had to put a large storage container under that. Sand was coming in with the rain. I put towels down everywhere and every fifteen minutes I had to get up and wring them out. I stayed wet all day.

Kat Ballou hid in the closet. I didn't see her all day. It continues to blow and rain all day. Things are flying across my roof, sometimes hitting the whirlygig with a bang. Every once in awhile I peek out the back door shutter to check on my Madeira tree; I don't want it to blow down. I bought it as a tiny tree at the first Friends of the Environment Fair. Fortunately, I didn't kill it, as I seem to do most plants.

I am not afraid of the storm but it is very frustrating.

The storm has slowed down and is almost stalled. I sit and worry about my trip to West Palm Beach on Tuesday to get my mammogram and then on to North Carolina for vacation. I was really looking forward to my trip as I hadn't been able to get away all year and my nerves seemed at a breaking point. Sometimes I would chew gum so I wouldn't keep my jaw clenched and this was making it worse as I remembered after Hurricane Floyd the airport was flooded for almost a week. Also, would I be able to leave my house? Would I be able to get it all dried out before then?

Just about midnight, the rain lets up and I find a small spot on my bed that I don't have piled up with something and curl up an doze off 'til daylight. At daylight, I get up and eat something then take a look outside. The wind has dropped down a lot. I take a walk with my camera. I walk along the inside of the ball field fence to go see the beach. I step in a knee-deep sinkhole and scratched my legs up. It try to go across the graveyard to the top of the sand dune but can't get halfway, the wind is still blowing the sand so hard it stings. I have a head and mouth full of sand and the rest of me is covered.

I walk up the street. Everyone is coming out and moving trees and fences so vehicles can pass. Everything is sandblasted. I walk towards the Hope Town Harbour Lodge but can't get past the Krouts' house because the sand is piled five feet high in the road there. I go behind the church to look at the beach. It is sheltered there so I could get far enough. There is bad erosion in that area but not as bad as Floyd. Down towards our area doesn't look as bad. I start towards home and meet people. Everyone seems to be okay. Reports from Marsh Harbour are that there is a lot of damage there and lots of water. The airport is under water. I wonder again if I will be able to get out of here on Tuesday. I go back home as another band of rain and strong winds are passing by. I wring more towels but the wind and rain soon let up. I have an early supper and go to bed. It has been an exhausting thirty-six hours.

I get up very early Sunday morning and sit by my front door. The wind has dropped way down and the sun comes out. I thank God for the sunshine. Kat Ballou ventures to the door and sees the sunshine and goes out at last. I wonder if there will be any church service this morning as I think about all the wet towels and carpet I have to put outside to dry. Vernon says there will be a 9:30 church service. I get myself together and dress and start for church. My watch is slow. I meet Vernon and Matt coming back and said nobody showed up. I go back home and start hanging out wet towels and putting out carpet to dry. Good thing my carpet is indoor/outdoor and is in 18" x 18" squares. I can only lift three of them at a time, dripping with water, but I get them all outside in the sun.

Vernon says he and Matt are going to the Lodge for lunch if I want to go with them. We go to the Lodge and everyone we meet says,

"Have you seen the coconut tree at *Sunrise Tellin*?"

On the way back, we stop at *Sunrise Tellin*. It's amazing that a tall coconut tree that was growing on the deck has blown over and is underneath the deck rail and all the rail is still in place. I guess it's one of the unexplained things that happen in a storm.

I go back home. Some towels are dry, making room to hang some more. I go to the graveyard to check on Benjie's grave and see Jeff Key there. He has just come from Man-O-War and said he saw my sister and everyone is okay. I feel better after that. Although I felt sure everyone was all right, there is still that deep down fear that maybe not. We have no phone communication to anywhere. I still worry about my sister and brother in Ft. Lauderdale as the storm is going that way.

Late Sunday afternoon, the guy on the boat with a sat phone comes ashore and I call my brother and he says they are all well and didn't have much wind but don't have any power. Haven't had any more rain, good thing because all the carpet from Benjie's room, half of mine and some from the living room are out in the yard.

I still wonder about getting out of here on Tuesday. I hear Marsh Harbour Airport has less than five feet of water.

It's Monday morning, my sister comes up from Man-O-War and we walk around town, then come back home and take off a couple of shutters so the house will dry out better. I take out my suitcase and clean it and put a few things in, most of my clothes I want to take are dirty. I will have to take them like that. I have enough clean to take to North Carolina and Cindy has a washer.

I clean out most of the things in my 'fridge; it isn't too cold anymore. Vernon couldn't get either generator to start this morning and I don't want to leave my power on while I'm away: I know water has leaked down into my outlets so I won't take a chance.

Small charter planes are flying into Marsh Harbour, the area is clear, but I can't find out if USAir is going to fly. Someone said Continental came in but maybe that's just a rumor.

Tuesday morning I get up early and finish packing my suitcase. Actually, I don't know exactly what I put in it. I had a few gifts to take but could only find a small book I had for Shirley. It got wet but I dried it out and took it anyway, a true Hurricane Frances souvenir. My cistern is full so I get some water and wash the salt out of my hair and take a spit bath. Our friend with the sat phone is ashore and we call USAir but they don't know if they are flying. Everyone says go to the airport anyway so we call the hotel to make sure they are open. They just opened the day before. I decide to go on the 11:30 ferry. Then Mark called and said USAir said they were flying so I get on the ferry. I get to Marsh Harbour and go to the airport. The main terminal is still under water but immigration and customs are at Cherokee Air so the taxi heads that way. I get there and check about my flight. They say they have been trying all day to get USAir agents to come out there but can't find them.

Faron must have seen the look of desperation on my face so he said don't leave, we'll find something. And so I sit, chewing gum to avoid clenching my jaws. Cherokee Air can't get hold of Customs or Immigration in Palm Beach so they can't fly there.

Two o'clock comes and no sign of any USAir agent or plane. Someone said, "Bud is coming; inform West Palm." Bud flies for Tank Ship Co. Bud comes in and I hear Faron say, "There's a lady here who wants to go."

Then Bud says, "Anybody who wants to go, I'll take them; just collect their departure tax." Bud says its rough out there. I thought for a minute but he said he had been flying for thirty years and if he will go, I will go.

So six of us got on the plane and took off. It was a beautiful plane, not a bit of pressure and quiet. There was just one spot of bumpy weather. We landed at Jet Aviation where we landed when we took Benjie after his accident. It brought back lots of memories.

The people there were very nice; they even called a taxi for me. I arrive at the hotel (known locally as The Abaco Inn because so many Abaconians stay there). Ron at the desk looks worn out and tired. They had just gotten power and opened the night before. Good thing I'd had a reservation, they said they could have sold three hundred rooms that day. I couldn't wait to get to my room to have a lovely warm bath and wash the sand out of my hair.

I went back out to the desk to check on somewhere to eat.

"Everything nearby is closed except the Chinese place across the street. The mall is closed; Target is closed; they have no electricity. And, there is a ten o'clock curfew." I wonder about the mammography centre; I'll try them in the morning.

Wednesday, I try calling the mammography centre and get no answer. I go out to the lobby and see my nephew and his friend there. They said they would take me there to check. I didn't want to spend $40 on a taxi if they weren't open. Sure enough, no one is there. We stop at a drugstore on the way back and get some toothpaste and something to read.

Next morning, I get on a plane to North Carolina. Shirley and Cindy meet me. They were glad to see me even with my dirty clothes.

October 2004

HURRICANE OF 2004
ONE PERSON'S PERSPECTIVE
Kitty Donnan

Everything goes black; I can't see my husband sitting next to me. Our connection to The Weather Channel is gone. Dave reaches for the flashlight then ignites candles waiting nearby for the call for duty. The flames quiver, an incongruous sweet aroma floats to my nose before I can turn away.

"It's going to be just fine," he says with a lilt, then peers through the window into a night as dark as a young child's room in a creaky house. 'Gracie,' our immaculate Subaru, has been forsaken under towering pines without even a cover over her gray body.

On a clear day, our rented cabin has a breathtaking view of six rows of mountains from a deck that teeters high into the treetops. We reach it in low gear on a one-lane dirt road that we slid back down on our first attempt. There is no telephone.

Before the sun went down, we peered under the house, as weather forecasters warned of flooding rivers, mud slides, winds of 90-100 miles per hour, and tornados. We are pretty sure the log house was not built to hurricane standards – who would even think of a hurricane visiting the mountains of North Georgia? Yet, here is Ivan, howling across the valley and onto the ridge, where we are the only people in residence.

It has been thirteen days since Hurricane Frances lingered over Abaco, wreaking havoc and leaving us feeling far away and helpless, while friends there struggled to pick up the pieces and carry on their lives. Reports from Hope Town were like the first words parents get from their child in a war zone, welcomed with an undercurrent of dread.

In morning's first light, we inspect Ivan's damage the pungent smell of pine fills the air. Dave gets one large tree off the road and together we chop branches from another that has become an archway, working until we achieve enough clearance to drive Gracie underneath – if we have to. Two days later we have power, just in time to pack up and head to Sarasota for a long-planned, three-day visit with our neighbors from home.

We find two other Abaco friends there, seeking shelter from Stuart, Florida where Hurricane Jeanne seems to be headed – after she leaves the Bahamas. Her path, after many days, leaves a footprint like a drunk's wanderings. First it was a cause for celebration, "It's headed away!" Then the realization it's turned back and Abaco in the bulls-eye position. We embrace the company of four who know how to pronounce Abaco, and know how unique and lovable it and its people are. Sarasota's foliage reminds us of what's at risk.

"I want to cancel our reservations for Munich; yes, for tomorrow evening." I reach to turn on the light; the sun has slipped beyond the horizon. I bite hard on my bottom lip and take a deep breath.

"Yes, I am still here. We just want to go home. The eye of the hurricane came right to the little island where we live, where our home is, our only home. We want to go home. Please help us."

The woman's voice is balm to my anxious soul.

"I'm truly sorry," she says softly.

The decision to cancel our trip to Bavaria – our postponed honeymoon trip, is not difficult. But it takes us a while to reach it, neither wanting to disappoint the other. When we find our voices, we both want exactly the same thing – to go home.

"Want to see downtown Marsh Harbour?" asks the young pilot of the small plane with seven apprehensive passengers.

"Yes," we answer in unison, as he dips a wing and circles around. Docks look as if an angry giant had picked them up and thrown them down in disgust. Standing water, blue tarps and stuff every place but the right place. When we climb from the plane the sun warms our arms and hearts. The taxi takes us past a live-aboard powerboat that came from the harbor and crossed the road before stopping in spitting distance of Sapodilly's deck.

"Uooow, a chain saw," a man at the ferry dock says to Dave, with envy in his eyes. The photo on the sturdy box doesn't depict how the user, soon to be Dave, looks after a full day of work, much less after several weeks. As we head to Elbow Cay my stomach ties and reties its knots. We leave eleven things on the dock and head home for wheelbarrows. It is very still and quiet; I try to make my eyes reach our house before we turn the corner.

"Oh no, that blob across the road on the internet picture, that was our fig tree," I wail.

"Not all of it – see, most of it is still standing," says my always-optimistic husband.

"It will grow back and fill in."

Everything is so brown, like a sepia photograph.

"What happened to all the leaves?" I'm a novice hurricane-er; I can't imagine the courage of those who have been through two in three weeks and are still walking and talking and working, working, working. As we get closer I see what happened to the leaves – we shuffle through them, and our pale yellow home is as speckled with brown as a potcake puppy.

"I'll have to get a broom first thing in the morning and sweep these off the house," I say to myself. But as I brush with my hand and scrape with my fingernails I realize the leaves are as firmly fixed as if they had been painted...with sand and salt coating every surface.

We drag wheelbarrows through the sand back to the dock, load our luggage and promptly have a flat tire - like the camel in the Hope Town Christmas play that refused to move...No, no this camel won't go.

Back home we take a quick look around and find water a foot deep in front of the golf cart garage and the laundry room, both below ground level. Dave scoops goopy leaves and sand from the drain covers but the water doesn't move. Sunset calls 'Time' before the job is finished. The generator starts like a mush dog eager to begin the Iditarod Race. Whew, that deep, loud rumbling is a sweet sound!

We sidle around the deck furniture stored in the living room, have something for dinner, washed down with Gatorade and fall into bed. The visions dancing in my head are not of sugarplums. Nonetheless, I am thrilled to be home and find it isn't as bad as we feared...and eager to tackle whatever will be revealed tomorrow.

The next morning we move two chairs and a small table onto the deck for our Gatorade and granola bar breakfast. I see there are a few green leaves. A penetrating smell, like a compost pile that's been turned greets us below a hopeful blue sky. On a walk into town I say to Trish, who was here for both hurricanes.

"Next year we aren't going away during the hurricane season. I'd rather be here and know than away worrying." She looks at me as if I am insane.

"Next year I'm going away. Maybe after I've forgotten what it's like, then I'll stay."

We begin to discover Frances and Jeanne's calling cards: blue stuff oozing from the golf cart plug with the verdict that the cart "may be reparable." It sat in a foot and a half of water. I notice one of the sheets covering furniture in the living room is pink - that's odd, we don't have any pink sheets. Then I see our red living room rug looks like a science project. Later, we scoop the mold from it with spatulas before lugging it out to the deck for serious cleaning. The TV dish dangles and the wind vane pointer is wrapped back and flattened against the flag side. Shingles litter the ground. Broken limbs are scattered and intertwined everywhere, like the first throw in a game of Pickup Stix. I open the dryer and discover it is half-full of water. We don't turn on the washer until an expert comes and certified is needs a heart and lung transplant. A downed gum elemi tree no longer holds up its end of the clothesline. After two days of swerving through the thickets of changed terrain and visiting with stalwarts who never left, we settle into a routine of early rising, work until sundown, turn on the generator, wash the grime off, have a "cleanup punch" of rum and room temperature Gatorade and dinner from a bag or a box, then sink into bed. Sleep is broken with images of things to do, balanced one on top of another and another and another.

I discover I have more physical than emotional energy. I forget things, find making conversation draining and dissolve into tears over the smallest thing. I'm a good worker but not easy to live with.

But I also find some can'ts turn into cans.

"I can't wash towels in a bucket," but I do.

"I can't possibly wash a sheet in this tiny bucket," but I can in a sink.

Patience has never been my long suit, but after trying everything else, I apply straight bleach on the drywall in the laundry room. Twenty minutes later the mold and mildew are still there...but after ten hours it is all gone. The sight of Bavarian Alps could not have been more pleasing than these clean, white walls.

After five weeks of experience, I am proud to say I became proficient at washing in buckets. Once, as I scrubbed, I felt eyes and when I screamed and clapped my hands, not a fur moved, convincing me he was dead. I stepped over him to pour buckets of wash water then rinse water on stubs of bougainvillea. When I was almost through – to heck with conservation – I poured the last bucket of rinse water down the sink drain. It bubbled up a drain near where he was hunkered down and he moved toward me. I jumped over him and ran upstairs to Dave. As a professed feminist, I am not proud to say I had to get my husband from his sickbed to help me with an Abaco Ground Squirrel.

Dave, less than a week after we arrived, had a bout of gout and was under doctor's orders to elevate his foot, which was as painful as a tooth being drilled without Novocain. He is a man who thrives on work...so my nagging to do what the doctor ordered was an irritation almost as bad as his incapacitation. Now, all of a sudden, I appear.

"Please, come downstairs. There is a mouse at the bottom of the step. If he were in a flat place, I'd take a broom and sweep him away. But I don't know what to do and he's cute and I can't bear to whack him with a shovel. I need your help."

Immediately, Dave is in action, pooh-poohing my suggestion that he put on some gloves. Before you could say "Mickey Mouse," he was back to tell me it was a rat, not a mouse and it won't bother me again. After that heroic action, I didn't nag for at least an hour.

I notice when I ask others how they are doing, the reply is often, "I'm fine," spoke through teeth clamped together

"I tell everyone, 'Don't be nice to me or I'll cry.'" Peggy says.

"I'm angry a lot," says another.

Ten days after we arrive, the power is restored and our spirits brighten. Week by week things happen. Our roof is repaired; a new washing machine delivered. We still have no telephone and the golf cart parts have yet to make the boat. In six weeks there is a transformation from brown to green. Dave uses the chainsaw and rake non-stop. Incredibly wonderful neighbors loan us their golf cart, telephone, shoulders and pick-up truck. The truck is not a thing of beauty. It is covered with more rust than paint, and has see-through floorboards. Plus, we now have views of both the ocean and the Sea of Abaco.

As I sat in church last Sunday, I thought of the piles of debris stacked everywhere on our damaged island. They remind me of funeral pyres. When they are burned there should be silence to honor the graceful palms that once swayed in silvery summer moonlight, the gum elemi, so like living sculptures whose berries enticed the birds, the hibiscus which gave sustenance to hummingbirds and butterflies, and even poisonwood, the only nesting place of white-crowned pigeons.

We should also remember docks that children scampered down before jumping into azure water, pilings which provided safe havens for boats, dock houses where life jackets hung, and boards where fish were cleaned in anticipation of a heavenly meal. Fences where people stopped to chat and trellises where yellow blossoms dangled. They served us well and will be missed.

At the end of silence, we should recognize that on the plants and trees that survived there is new growth at the broken places. Perhaps, given time, the same can be said for us.

P.S. November 12, after six weeks and two days, our golf cart "Tillie the Toiler" is home. November 13, after six weeks and three days, our telephone and internet service is restored. It has been a BIG 24 hours for which we are thankful!

November 2004

SATURDAY AT HOME
(NINE WEEKS AFTER HURRICANE JEANNE)
Mary Balzac

Still bleaching mildew, painting trim. .
Scrubbing, scraping clinging leaf bits.
Watching buds grow to white flowers
To tiny green peppers in container deck garden.
Enlarging daily toward eating size.

Purple tinged flowers on ends of
Straw-thin green beans growing
Longer and fatter toward picking time.
Young kale and tasty chard
In salads and sandwiches.   .

Hibiscus and Yellow Elder blooming,
Gum elemies in luxuriant new growth,
Five key limes cling obstinately as
Dead seeming branches return to life.
Grapefruit trees struggle. May be a lost cause.

Hummingbird feeders brim full
Banana quits were waiting when I arrived,
Too busy to notice their need
They left. I await their return.
I have yet to see a hummingbird.

I must to the store for Christmas cookie ingredients.

November 2004

MOTHER NATURE'S CLEANING TEAM:
FRANCES AND JEANNE
Maureen Miller

Mother Nature cleaned house again
Giving hair cuts to various trees
Pruning back the dead wood
And shaving off the leaves

Bowing roofs from dwellings
Shoving boats against the shore
Washing all with torrential rains
Cleaning to the core

Mother Nature cleaned house again
With water from frothy seas
Scrubbing all with blown sand
Mainland, islands and cays

Destructive, some folks call her task
Vicious and somewhat mean
But there's method beyond her madness here
Effects yet to be seen

Mother Nature cleaned house again
Clearing out the views
Discarding stuff right and left
No questions as to whose

Frenzied, some would call her pace
Indiscriminate and truly brash
Sweeping wildly left and right
Leaving mounds of trash

Mother Nature cleaned house again
Plowing a frightful path
But we've emerged gratefully
In the aftermath

Grateful that she spared our lives
And those of ones we love
Grateful that she's loosed the sun
In clean blue skies above

Grateful that she's bringing back
Green leaves and flowers fair
Grateful that she's calm again
After giving such a scare

Mother Nature cleaned house again
A chore performed infrequently
To remind those of us within her realm
Of our fragility

December 2004

STUART, FLORIDA MAKES HURRICANE HISTORY
Mary Balzac

Returning from last minute shopping, I found Dolores pulling out the metal hurricane shutter strips she had put away after uncovering her windows less than three weeks previously, after the passing of Hurricane Frances.

"You might as well unpack, Mary. We won't be driving to Palm Beach International tomorrow. Jeanne has taken a sudden turn to the west and headed straight for Abaco on her way to Stuart."

"What? No way. You've got to be kidding," I said as I put down my packages.

"While you were out, I turned on the noon news on Channel 10. I'm not sure I quite believe it yet myself. I suggest we watch The Weather Channel tropical update just to be sure and then go out and do some hurricane marketing before the crowds gather. Also, I want to top off the gas tank."

As we watched the tropical update, the news sank in; I would not be going home tomorrow. I would be sitting here waiting along with my sister for the arrival of Hurricane Jeanne. I still didn't want to believe it, wanting instead to believe it would turn north.

"Okay, let's go shopping." Later, we watched the Channel 10 news at five o'clock as the weatherman explained the weather patterns affecting the storm that caused it to turn in our direction. He made true believers of us.

Dolores called her friend Mary O'Hara, another widow, who lives in the same complex in a second floor condo facing the river, to invite her to stay for the duration of the storm in Dolores's more secure location on the first floor away from the water. Mary spent two nights with Dolores during the long passage of Hurricane Frances. They were able to keep the front door open during most of that storm, moved the dining table into the hallway once the electricity went off and sat there doing handwork while they watched the wind and the rain blow by from north to south and then from south to north. After the storm, they survived their five days without power quite well for two almost-eighty-year-old ladies.

As the winds started to pick up the next day, we watched the weather channel religiously, only flipping over to Channel 10 for the hourly reports. Cha had called from Marsh Harbour; she let us know that people we knew, including Victor Patterson, were being interviewed by The Weather Channel. I caught a glimpse of: Victor putting up his hurricane shutters once again, the Solomon Bros. Superstore, happenings at a local shelter and Silbert Mills and Cay Russell being interviewed. My mind was more at ease once I knew Lory and Thomas were holing up in her house; Jane, Erin and Ben with Pattie Love and family at Clifford Sawyer House in town; and Cha, Frank, Aly and James with Brenda and Eleanor and one of their neighbors, a young man involved with the new development at Winding Bay, in their sturdy home on Pelican Shores. We continued to keep a close watch on the weather news and took a walk out to view the swelling river waters and the gathering clouds as the first rain bands moved in. Cha said she'd call on their friend Chad's satellite phone just as soon as she could. Mary will join us just as soon as the winds picks up a bit more. Her bed is made.

"Oh my God! Dolores, come quick. The Weather Channel is showing Marsh Harbour during the eye. It's flooded on Front Street and there are big boats up on land! The wind must have come right down the harbor!"

Our winds are picking up. Mary comes through the door with her overnight case and dinner and snacks in hand. Time to put up the last of the shutters on the kitchen window and bedroom facing the parking lot. Mary hands the panels to Dolores as I shoot a digital to record the moment. Mary smiles and in her lilting Irish accent quotes from Macbeth, "When shall we three meet again in thunder, lightning and in rain?" It's nice to have her bright optimism with us. We settle in as the storm intensifies, eat our dinner and play a few sets of Rummikub.

Night descends; the storm strengthens. Cha calls as our lights flicker on and off and on again. In a high pitched and shaking voice,

"We're all okay. We're all okay, the house is okay, though it leaked like a sieve because of the Frances damage, but the water came under the house again, like in Floyd. Everything is ruined again!"

The lights flicker on and off and I wish they would just stay off!

"Oh, Cha, just as long as you are all okay. That's what matters. I love you. I'll call everyone on the list you gave me. Call again as soon as you can!"

The lights finally go off.

I don't sleep. Mary, the optimist, goes off to bed. Dolores and I sit up listening to the excellent coverage by the weathermen of Channel 10. Dolores finally gives in and goes to her room but I know she has the radio on low and isn't sleeping. I lie down on the couch but sleep doesn't come. Does that hurricane shutter door over the window wall with the sliding glass door really work? These winds are more intense than they were in Frances. I sit up and listen to the voice of the reporter on the radio and silently bless him for the calm he is exuding. I breathe deep and will my self to stay calm. Memories from thirty plus years ago of the bowing window wall on our front room during Hurricane Betsy flood my mind.

"Okay now, here's the latest for you folks north of us," the reporter says from West Palm Beach.

"It looks like two more rain bands before the eye. The first is strong, a deep red on the radar screen. It's coming down through Stuart now and this is followed by what looks to be a lesser one and then you'll have the eye. If I'm correct, it looks like another Stuart landfall."

I sit and listen. I feel the building vibrate, more deep breathing. Moments later, I notice the wind lessening. Dolores comes out. We open the front door. It is the middle of the night and all is calm. We take a walk out into the complex. The parking lot isn't flooded. Water is still draining easily. We walk through the hall between buildings to look out toward the pool area. There is high water in the cement walk way between the buildings. It is misty out over the river. We decide it is too dark to venture further. The quiet is welcome. When the eye passes and the other side of the storm starts to blow, I realize it isn't as bad now and finally to go to bed and get a few hours of sleep.

In the morning, while drinking a Coke (I want my caffeine; Dolores has an electric stove) we hear on the radio that Jeanne made landfall at the House of Refuge on Hutchinson Island about two miles from the Sewall's Point arrival of Frances less than three weeks earlier. Stuart makes history as the first place two major storms had come ashore so close together within so short a period of time. Dolores looks at me with a knowing look and a slight smile.

While I was still in Washington State while Frances was traveling, I had, to me, a rather sudden and surprising vision of the House of Refuge and had told Dolores so when I called to see what preparations she was making. We hoped I wasn't prophesizing that the House of Refuge was going to be destroyed after so many years facing out to sea. Once a haven for shipwrecked sailors it is now a museum. The House of Refuge stood through Frances. A picture in the paper showed the fence in front blown over and the sand gone from Bathtub Beach in front of it. The House of Refuge also stood through Hurricane Jeanne. Just south of it, a ¼-mile, four-foot deep opening was cut through Hutchinson Island from the Atlantic to the Indian River inland waterway causing residents of Sailfish Point on the southern tip of the island to resort to ferry service provided by the City of Stuart until further notice.

October 2004

WITCHY WOMEN
Steve Best

My parents told me that I experienced my first hurricane at the age of two, in Miami. I don't count this as an experience as I slept through the entire storm, even as our neighbors' roof was being torn from their house.

I found it hard to believe that I never awoke, except until two generations later, when my daughter, Sabra, and her two year-old child, Madison, experienced Hurricane Hazel in Hope Town. That storm blew at about 100 miles per hour until it left near dusk. The following morning we found that our right-of-way was littered with fallen trees and debris that had not been there when we went to bed. The hurricane had returned from the west that night with greater force and each of us had slept through it.

My first hurricane in Hope Town was Erin, in the early nineties, which blew with about the same force as Hazel. There had been a rental mix-up and I left our oceanfront house, Skyward, and stayed in the Higgs' house on the Sea of Abaco. On the first evening, our caretaker, Carrie Cash, called to say that Erin was to arrive on the following day and we needed to put up the shutters on Skyward. Dutifully, Didi and I, along with our two Jack Russell terriers, walked up to the house and complied, as our tenants were retiring to bed. It was a gorgeous night and we walked back along the beach as the calm sea glistened beneath the moon. How incongruous to realize that soon a terrifying storm might ravage our peaceful island. Carrie must be mistaken.

On the following morning we walked into the village on what seemed to be a normal day. Even as we reached Vernon's Store, the wind was brisk but not fierce. I decided to walk up to the beach and have a look. As I reached the top of the dune, an imaginary door opened on an entirely different world. The beach had disappeared and as the ocean crashed against the dune, it appeared out of focus. Gone were the blues and greens, replaced by a purplish grey interrupted by continuous breakers. I had to lean forward to remain standing and my body was being strafed by sand and water although I was some thirty feet above sea level and it was not raining. I gazed in awe at an eerie beauty. Winslow Homer would probably have pulled up a chair and begun painting, as he had done at his home in Prout's Neck, Maine. I elected to record the sight in my memory and wait until the storm passed.

We spent much of the day viewing the storm in the lee of the Cashes' porch, watching boats in the harbor tugging at their leashes, straining constantly from one side to the other, as sails were ripped into shreds. The other end of the harbor was barely visible. Still, you could walk down the Queen's Highway in relative comfort.

The eye of the hurricane passed through before noon, and for more than an hour it was quiet and sunny. When Hazel returned from the west, the Cash porch became uninhabitable, but the hurricane lost much of its fury. When it had dissipated, we decided to go up and se how our tenants were doing. No one was there and we walked in to see how Skyward had fared.

Immediately to the left was the ocean-side bathroom where the windows had been left cracked. Both the bed and the floor were sopping wet. Upstairs it was the same. We began soaking up water with towels, wringing them out, and repeating the process. After about an hour, our three tenants returned and one of them (I shall call her the Witchy Woman) demanded to know what we were doing in their house. She then recognized me as the same person who had disturbed their sleep the night before.

We learned that in the morning they decided to ride out the hurricane with friends who were renting a house on the harbor. They didn't figure they needed to shut the windows tight as the shutters were up. Living in hurricane land, one soon learns that sand and water will find a way to gain access to your house in ways you cannot imagine. The only question is how much. We left our tenants with indisputable evidence of this fact.

Dawn arose on a day as lovely as the one two days before. Knowing we would not like to sit inside a house shuttered from the outside, we decided to show mercy and returned to Skywards after breakfast, where we quietly removed the shutters from the doors leading out to the main deck. Afterward, we dropped by the Cashes' for a cup of coffee, only to learn that the Witchy Woman had just called to complain.

"That nasty man is back, with his two nasty dogs."

I shook my head and laughed.

"How dare she call my dogs nasty? I think I'll go back and put the shutters back up." Didi overruled me.

When the tenants left after their week was up, the Witchy Woman said their rent should be returned in full. We overruled her. I have not seen her back on the island since. Hurricanes can't be all bad.

People, as well as animals react differently to hurricanes. One of my dogs would run into the broom closet for the duration. The other would run outside and bark in fury. I am somewhere in between. My general conclusion is that I like hurricanes more when they are going on than when they are over. Had I been here for Floyd, the mother (or father) of all Bahamian hurricanes, I might have felt differently. Still, I will never forget returning days after it left and seeing not one touch of green, just brown and devastation everywhere. Going through Irene days later was almost a relief, as the wind and rain brought a promise of life to what had seemed a quiet death.

That was the time we were awakened by the barking of our dogs; something was amiss. We looked out on what seemed to be a glorious sunset over Hope Town, but why near midnight? It had rained hard that night but not now. A fire was raging, fueled by a southerly wind that threatened to spread it through the entire north end of the settlement. Hope Town faced a devastation no hurricane could ever accomplish. People appeared from everywhere, risking personal safety to rescue their village from destruction, but it appeared grim. Then miraculously, the wind died down and it began to rain once again. Three houses were totally destroyed and several others were damaged but Hope Town was spared. Hurricanes are terrible, but there are worse calamities. In fact more people are killed in accidents by the few vehicles on Elbow Cay than by hurricanes.

Frances must have been hellish because it lasted so long. Normally, a hurricane passes through in eight hours or so, and at times I think I might prefer an eight-hour hurricane to the occasions when the wind blows a steady thirty knots for days on end, with no excitement and no variation.

I love Skyward more than any material object I've ever had. I intend to finish my life here, although I'm in no hurry. It was sad to return once more, after Frances, and to see it ravaged by sand and sea and rain, once more to begin the drudgery of cleaning up and repairing, day after day, week after week.

I learned that the wind blew from easterly directions at one hundred miles an hour or more for thirty-six hours. Shutters which held through the much stronger winds during Floyd were gradually worn away until they broke free, leaving wing bolts intact on their screws. In other spots, the incessant wind slowly loosened shutters which rattled until they pulled three-inch screws out of pressure-treated wood, followed soon by broken windows and the rush of sand and water, spreading like hordes of tiny ants. Floors became beaches. Multiple coats of paint on walls disappeared, replaced by grains of sand which became imbedded like the pebbledash one purposely placed on houses but now extinct because it is so labor-intensive. Not so for a hurricane. It can pebbledash your house in no time.

My yard is a foot higher than when I left, covered by a beige snow that will not melt. I used to descend two steps from my deck to the sand; now, I must step up. The only palm fronds remaining on trees are brown, drooping vertically in apparent sorrow. I feel like Lawrence of Arabia without an oasis, but I know the oasis will return.

I awake each day at dawn as my Haitian-for-hire arrives and together we work until dusk. He will earn more money in one day than his father in Haiti can earn in one year and he will send most of it back home. I have no regrets. When the old bones begin to stiffen, the magnificent ocean will beckon me for a quick dip and they will be healed. I will have dinner with friends at the Harbour Lodge and we will exchange war stories. I will sleep well, arise again and repeat the day before but with less sand inside and more outside. The power is back on and the accustomed comforts begin returning. The worst day in Hope Town is better than the best day in rush-hour traffic as there is not such thing.

Then we learn that we will soon have an unexpected guest who has been cruising the Atlantic aimlessly for about a week. Her name is Jeanne and she has decided to drop by, perhaps on the recommendation of Frances. So, shutters we have just taken down go back up and new shutters are made to replace those now gone with the wind. Now I feel like Snoopy cursing the Red Baron; I'm sticking around this time and you won't get me.

Hurricanes come in five categories. Suddenly I received a Category 6 shock. Carrie Cash and Jane Patterson arrive at my door to report a phone call from the States. Didi's son, Michael, has been killed in a freak accident. It comes like a sonic boom. No longer are hurricanes a horror; this is a horror. Less than an hour later I'm on a chartered ferry to Marsh Harbour.

There are worse demons than Jeanne. She can do what she wants. After all, it's only a house.

November 2004

BEYOND THE REEF

Eulogy to Abject Rejection
Mary Balzac

Little boy held baby hummingbird
Tiny wings outspread in palm of hand
Harming not a feather on its miniscule head.

Grown up to be a man, he shot
At Constable Malone in his home
(A bullet actually singed his ear).

In the next moment as noise
And gun smoke cleared,
He shot himself, now dead, instead.

April 2004

THE HALF-DOZEN WAYS
Don Weiner

Sad Lilly's now gone,
With the half-dozen ways,
Her porch-bound world,
Somehow lightened our days.

Our Lilly's now gone,
With the half-dozen ways,
Three dozen cat children,
Came purring her praise.

Mad Lilly's now gone,
With her shouts and her smoke,
And the half-dozen ways,
To the butt of a joke.

But on Lilly's front door,
Half-dozen roses now speak,
To our loss at her leaving,
And the solace we seek...

February 2002

Ode to Lilly
In memory of Lilly Bethel
1941-2002
Mary Balzac

Most mornings on the steps of the old weathered gray house
Next to the grocery store and across from Bethel's dock
Where the children gather to await the school ferry's arrival,
Lilly sat with her orange and white cats
On the cement steps below her rickety porch
Smoking a cigarette as she watched the world go by.

Passing on my way to work, my morning "Hello, Lilly",
Was acknowledged with a tentative nod or quiet raspy hello,
And I wondered what thoughts were appearing in her fear filled mind.

Today, three long stemmed orange-red rose buds adorn her shuttered door
On cement steps red and magenta bougainvillea blossoms lie still.
Orange and white cats gather on the rickety wood porch eating
The dry food sprinkled there by Lisa. Orange and white cats lie
On the blossom-covered steps. Lilly is not there to greet.

One cat lies, head hanging over the edge of a step, its stomach
Rising and falling in little jerks. I wonder, is it sick or possibly expressing grief?
As I continue to watch, this orange and white cat stretches,
Pulls up its head, curls into a ball, and sleeps.

February 2002

ABACO HAIKU
Ann Corbitt

Rose dawn at sea's end
Clabber clouds dim the last thin
Slice of waning moon.

January 2002

INDEX

Works are listed alphabetically by author and in order of appearance.